ARIZONA
WAy OuT wESt&WACKy

AWESOME ACTIVITIES, HUMOROUS HISTORY, AND FUN FACTS

BY CONRAD J. STORAD & LYNDA EXLEY

Illustrated by Michael Hagelberg

FSC
www.fsc.org

MIX
Paper from
responsible sources
FSC® C002589

Little Five Star

THIS BOOK IS DEDICATED...

...to Arizona's elementary school teachers, some of the hardest working people I know.
Don't give up. We need you more than ever! —CJS

...to Marshall Trimble, for making my college Arizona history textbook
so interesting and fun that it inspired me to do the same for the younger crowd,
and to all those kids out there who "think" they don't like history! —LE

...to my Dad, an Arizona science and mathematics educator for 30 years,
now part of history. —MH

...to my Mother, Ann (Weiss) Foster, who with great courage and tenacity packed up
four children ages 13, 11, 9 and 7 and moved from a decaying steel town in the Midwest
to Phoenix back in 1960. She wanted us to grow up with greater opportunities.
So I dedicate this to her: a woman who had the foresight, courage and strength
to give us room to grow and dream in this great state of Arizona.
This legacy is now passed on to my children. —LFR

Linda F. Radke, President, Five Star Publications Inc.,
P.O. Box 6698, Chandler, AZ 85246-6698, 480-940-8182

www.AZWOWW.com

Publisher's Cataloging-In-Publication Data

Storad, Conrad J.

Arizona, way out west & wacky : awesome activities, humorous history and fun facts /
by Conrad J. Storad & Lynda Exley ; illustrated by Michael Hagelberg.

  p. : ill. ; cm.

Designated an Arizona Centennial Legacy Project by the Arizona Historical Advisory Commission.

ISBN-13: 978-1-58985-047-7
ISBN-10: 1-58985-047-5

1. Arizona–History–Juvenile literature. 2. Arizona–History. 3. Amusements.
I. Exley, Lynda. II. Hagelberg, Michael. III. Title. IV. Title: Arizona, way out west and wacky

F811.3 .S76 2011
979.1   2011935238

10 9 8 7 6 5 4 3 2

Editors: Conrad J. Storad, Lynda Exley
Book Design: Michael Hagelberg
Illustration: Michael Hagelberg

Printed in the United States of America
The text of this book is set in ITC Cheltenham.

CONTENTS

A Wild & Wacky WELCOME

HOWDY KIDS! My name is Johnny Ringo. You can call me JR for short. I'm here with my sister, Jayne, to share some wild and wacky things about Arizona. In case you hadn't noticed, I'm a Ringtail Cat. But, scientists prefer to call me just Ringtail. The folks at the state capitol made me the official state mammal in 1986.

☆ Way back in the 1800s, prospectors called ringtails like me a Miner's Cat. They treated me like a pet. I kept them company while they dug in the ground for gold, silver, and copper. We even chased mice and rodents away from the miner's food. To be honest, though, I'm not really a cat. My closest kin is the raccoon. ☆ Jayne and I will make discovering Arizona fun by telling stories about some of the craziest things that happened right here in the state. You'll see our pictures throughout this book. Color us! And try out the other coloring pages, puzzles, and activities. ☆ We promise that Arizona's history will amaze and amuse you!

TANTALIZING TOPOGRAPHY

GEOGRAPHY IS THE STUDY of all the physical features of the Earth's surface. Topography is what we call features on the surface of an area of land. In Arizona, there are plenty of different landforms of all shapes and sizes. Geographers and geologists have lots of fun here. But it took millions of years for the bits and pieces of Arizona to form into what we see today. ☆ Arizona is a huge place. In fact, it's the sixth largest state. It covers 113,635 square miles. That's 294,315 square kilometers for you fans of the metric system. ☆ Scientists divide Arizona into three main regions: plateau, mountain, and desert. The Colorado Plateau dominates the northeastern part of the state. It's made of lots of flat land, gorges, mountains, and valleys. The Painted Desert, Black Mesa, and Monument Valley are beautiful places in this part of Arizona. ☆ Of course, Arizona is called the Grand Canyon State because of the amazing canyon that winds through the state's northwest corner. The Grand Canyon was carved deep into the land by wind and water over millions of years. The canyon is 277 river miles long.

Watch out for ravens if you take a raft trip down the Colorado River through the Grand Canyon. The big black birds are notorious camp thieves. They will open backpacks to look for food and shiny jewelry. Scientists think that ravens may be among the smartest of all birds. But they are gross as well. Ravens will eat almost anything, dead or alive. They love to pluck out the eyes and pick the rotting meat off the bones of dead animals.

Arizona's Sonoran Desert is not a scrubland filled with rocks and sand dunes. It is a living desert. Except for the tropical rainforests of South America or Africa, the Sonoran Desert is home to more kinds of plants and animals than any other area of its size on Earth!

The deepest point
of the Grand Canyon is 6,000 feet.
The average female teacher is 5 feet,
4 inches tall. That means it would
take about 1,125 teachers standing
on each other's heads to go from
the bottom to the top!

It's one mile deep. It's 18 miles across at its widest point. The Colorado River runs through the heart of the Grand Canyon. The river forms Arizona's western border with Nevada and California. Other big rivers in Arizona include the Little Colorado, Verde, Gila, and Salt. ☆ Different ranges of the Rocky Mountains wind through Arizona. All are covered with trees of many kinds. To the north are the San Francisco Peaks. Humphrey's Peak is the highest point in Arizona. It soars 12,633 feet above the city of Flagstaff. To the east are the White Mountains. The Black Mountains rise in the northwest. ☆ The land flattens a bit as you move south toward Phoenix and the center of Arizona. But only a bit. There are plenty of mountains and canyons in the middle as well. Look for rust-colored peaks in the rugged terrain of the Big Horn, Gila, and Superstition Mountains. ☆ Farther south and west, the land is filled with the boulders, shrubs, and cactus-covered expanse of the beautiful

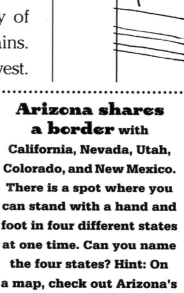

Arizona shares a border with **California, Nevada, Utah, Colorado, and New Mexico. There is a spot where you can stand with a hand and foot in four different states at one time. Can you name the four states? Hint: On a map, check out Arizona's northeast corner.**

Sonoran Desert. Go farther east toward Tucson and up rise the Rincon, Tucson, Santa Rita, and Santa Catalina Mountain ranges. The rugged peaks of the Chiricahua Mountains dominate the southeast corner of the state. Large sand dunes form in the southwest part near Yuma. ☆ In Arizona, you can see it all. There are mountains, canyons, rivers, extinct volcanoes, sand dunes, plateaus, forests, and cactus deserts. But one thing is always true: Arizona is a stunningly beautiful place.

Humphrey's Peak is the highest point in Arizona at 12,633 feet. It can be seen from almost anywhere in Flagstaff. There are 10 differences between the two pictures. Circle them. Can you find all 10?

THE SUN ALWAYS SHINES

HOT. COLD. DRY. A LOT OF EACH IN ARIZONA. Well, almost always. Yuma, Arizona is the sunniest city in the United States. The sun shines on more than 328 days of every year in Yuma. Phoenix, Tucson, and Flagstaff also rank among the top 10 sunniest cities every year. Yuma is also very dry. It is the driest city in America. In Yuma, it only rains an average of 17 days each year. The city gets just a bit more than 2.6 inches of rain each year. ☆

Arizona is the fourth driest state. Average rainfall is less than 14 inches each year. Of course, heat often comes hand in hand with sunny days. Despite all those sunny days, Arizona only ranks as the 10th hottest state. The average temperature on any day anywhere in Arizona is 60.3 degrees, Fahrenheit. ☆ But remember, that number is just the "average" temperature. It really does get HOT in Arizona. Sometimes it gets VERY HOT. In June 1994, the temperature soared to 128 degrees in Lake Havasu City. That is the second hottest temperature ever recorded in the United States. ☆ Phoenix is one of the hottest cities in the summer. The average temperature in July is 104 degrees. The temperature climbs above 100 degrees about 89 days of every year. ☆ Arizona is not hot everywhere all the time. Flagstaff is just 150 miles to the north of Phoenix. It is the eighth snowiest city in America. In Flagstaff, almost 100 inches of snow fall every year.

Can you fry eggs

on the sidewalk? You betcha! On a hot summer day in Phoenix, the temperature just above a concrete sidewalk can climb to more than 140 degrees, F. Parking lots made of asphalt can melt and get kind of gooey.

Arizona gets cold, too.

The coldest temperature ever recorded in Arizona was at Hawley Lake in the White Mountains. On January 7, 1971, the temperature plunged to 40 degrees below zero. In Phoenix, the coldest temperature ever was 16 degrees, set on January 7, 1913.

SILLY WEATHER JOKES

Once you've completed the three puzzles below, each phrase you figure out will complete this sentence:

It's so hot in Arizona that....

How it works: A fallen phrase puzzle shows the spaces for each word and letter in a phrase. Although they are scrambled, letters that appear directly below a column of spaces fit in one letter per space in that particular column. We solved the first one to show you how.

Notice in the first column there are only two spaces and two letters, E and R. The second column has only three spaces and three letters, and so on. It is your job to figure out which order the letters go in so they complete the phrase. Now you solve the next two.

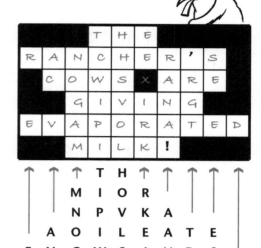

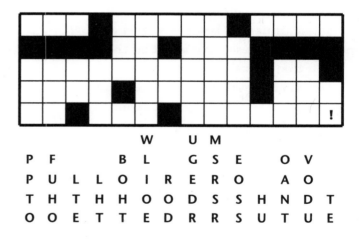

				T	H					
			T	H	O					
			M	I	R					
			N	P	V	K	A			
	A	O	I	L	E	A	T	E		
E	V	G	W	S	I	N	R	S		
R	C	A	C	H	E	R	G	E	D	

						W		U	M				
P	F			B	L		G	S	E			O	V
P	U	L	L	O	I	R	E	R	O			A	O
T	H	T	H	H	O	O	D	S	S	H	N	D	T
O	O	E	T	T	E	D	R	R	S	U	T	U	E

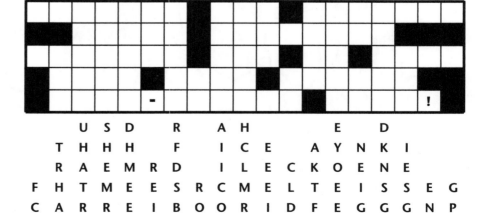

	U	S	D		R		A	H			E		D		
T	H	H	H		F		I	C	E		A	Y	N	K	I
R	A	E	M	R	D		I	L	E	C	K	O	E	N	E
F	H	T	M	E	E	S	R	C	M	E	L	T	E	I	S	S	E	G
C	A	R	R	E	I	B	O	O	R	I	D	F	E	G	G	N	P

What is a dust devil?

Dust devils look like miniature tornadoes.
But they are very different. Dust devils begin
when patches of ground get very hot.
The air above the ground heats up, too.
The heated air rises. It bangs together and
begins to spin. The result is a whirling column
of air that sucks up dirt and dust.
Dust devils can grow hundreds of feet tall.
The fastest dust devils spin at about
40 miles per hour.

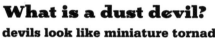

FANGS, STINGERS, STICKERS & THICK SKIN

ONE THING IS FOR CERTAIN, Arizona is a dry place. Scientists use the word *arid*. That means it just does not rain very much in Arizona, no matter which part you visit. Parts of Arizona can get very hot. Other parts get very cold. Some might call that a harsh environment. It's true; Arizona can be a rugged place to live.

☆ Believe it or not, plants and critters of all kinds live just fine in Arizona. But they have to be tough. Lots of Arizona plants have small waxy leaves. Others have thick skin, thorns, stickers, and spines. Some have roots that look like shallow nets. Others have a single large root that works like a straw. They slurp as much moisture as possible after rare rain showers. Many plants can survive without water for long stretches of time. ☆ The Arizona animals are just as tough. Some never drink water at all. They have adapted to deal with extreme temperatures. Many are nocturnal. These creatures rest during the hot days and are most active during the cooler nights. Some of the toughest have fangs, stingers, venom, and thick skin as well. Read on to learn more about a few of Arizona's roughest and toughest plants and critters.

Arizona's Sonoran Desert
has more species of rattlesnakes than anywhere else in world. Eleven different kinds of rattlers make their home in the desert. Overall, Arizona is home to 13 different types of rattlesnakes. Some scientists say there are even more species than that. Aren't we lucky?

FASTEST RUNNING FLYING BIRD Roadrunners don't say *meep meep*. And they don't look like a cartoon ostrich with a bad hairdo. But a roadrunner really is the world's fastest running flying bird. In Arizona, roadrunners also prefer running to flying. The speedy birds have been clocked zipping across the desert at speeds up to 15 miles per hour. Roadrunners grow to about the size of a skinny chicken. But they are tough hombres. They will actually fight a small rattlesnake. The winner gets to eat dinner.

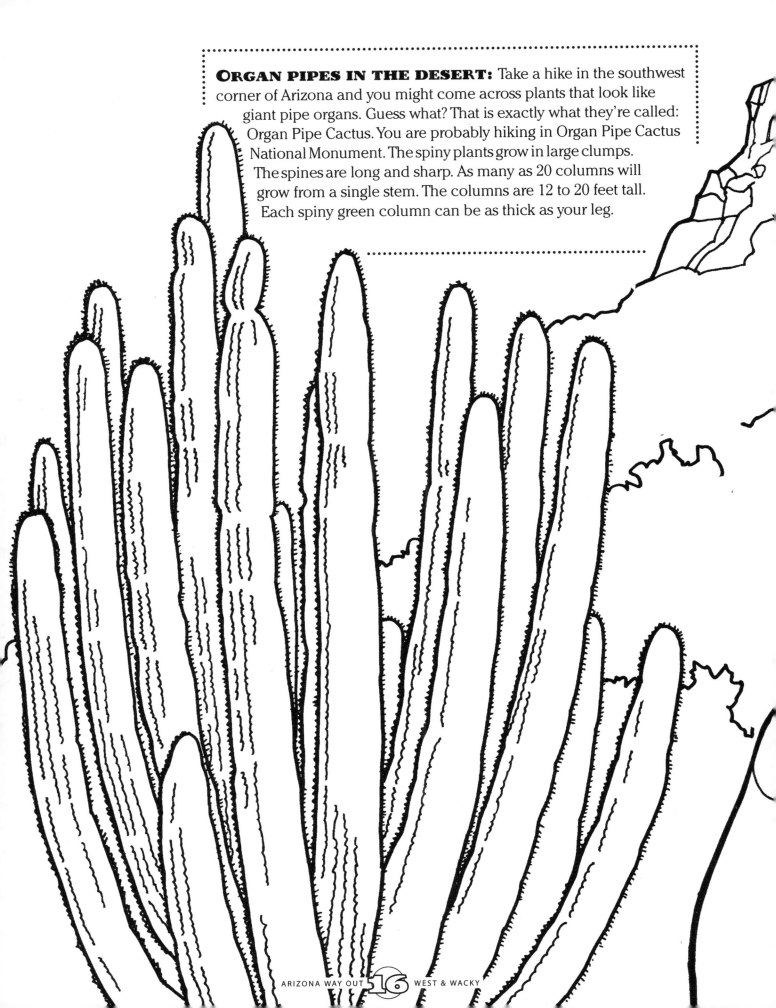

ORGAN PIPES IN THE DESERT: Take a hike in the southwest corner of Arizona and you might come across plants that look like giant pipe organs. Guess what? That is exactly what they're called: Organ Pipe Cactus. You are probably hiking in Organ Pipe Cactus National Monument. The spiny plants grow in large clumps. The spines are long and sharp. As many as 20 columns will grow from a single stem. The columns are 12 to 20 feet tall. Each spiny green column can be as thick as your leg.

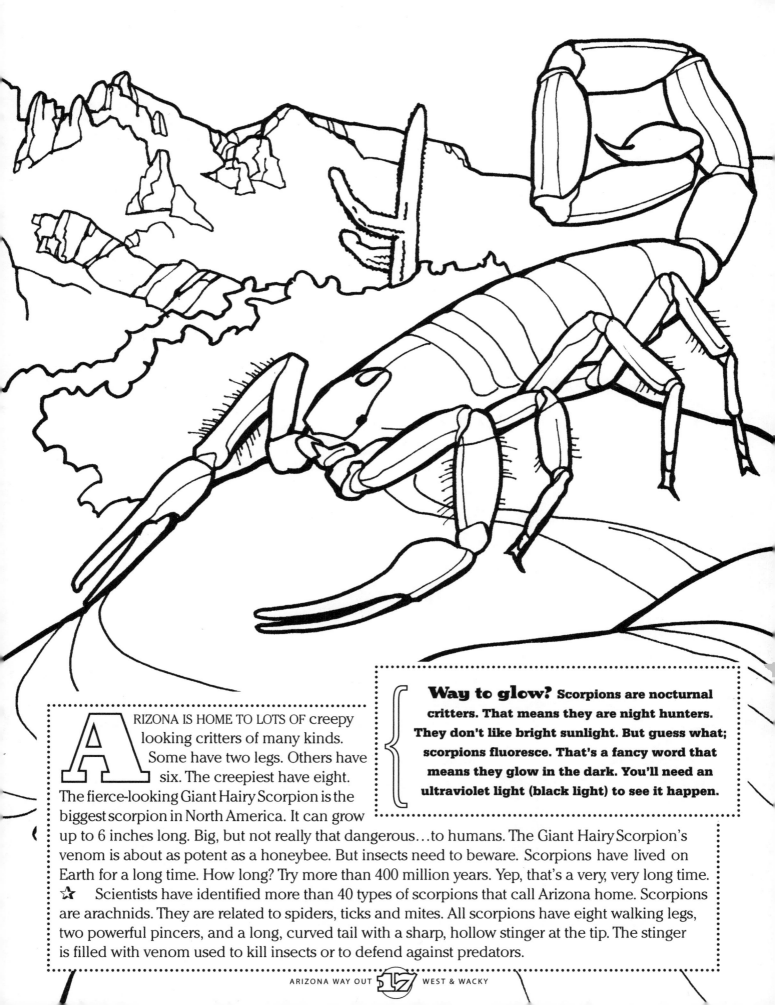

ARIZONA IS HOME TO LOTS OF creepy looking critters of many kinds. Some have two legs. Others have six. The creepiest have eight. The fierce-looking Giant Hairy Scorpion is the biggest scorpion in North America. It can grow up to 6 inches long. Big, but not really that dangerous…to humans. The Giant Hairy Scorpion's venom is about as potent as a honeybee. But insects need to beware. Scorpions have lived on Earth for a long time. How long? Try more than 400 million years. Yep, that's a very, very long time.

☆   Scientists have identified more than 40 types of scorpions that call Arizona home. Scorpions are arachnids. They are related to spiders, ticks and mites. All scorpions have eight walking legs, two powerful pincers, and a long, curved tail with a sharp, hollow stinger at the tip. The stinger is filled with venom used to kill insects or to defend against predators.

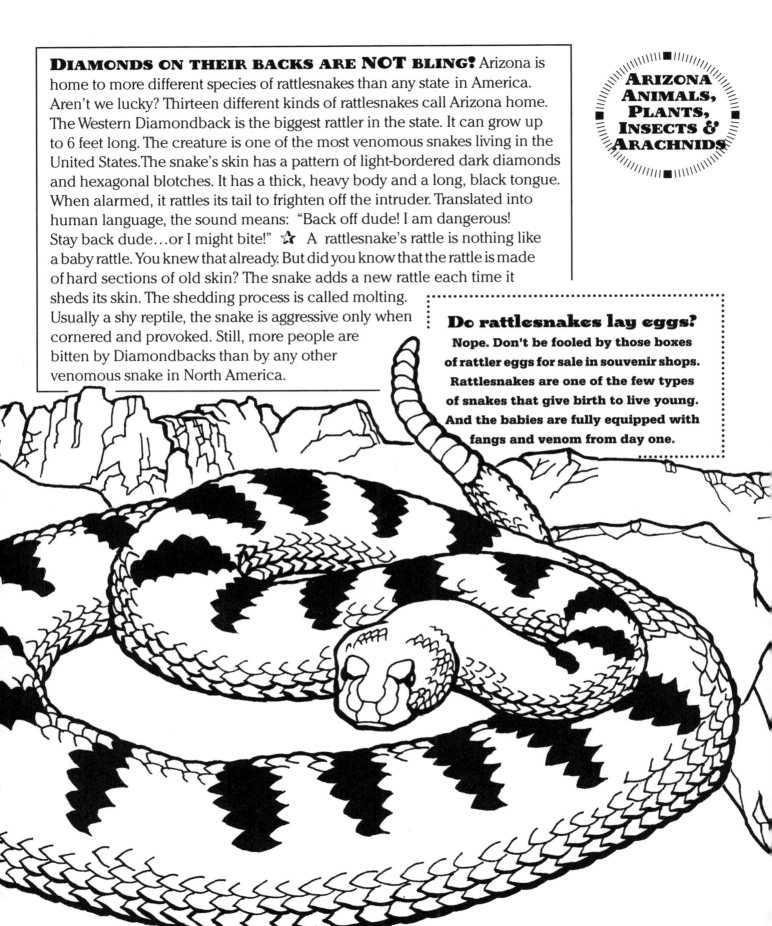

DIAMONDS ON THEIR BACKS ARE NOT BLING! Arizona is home to more different species of rattlesnakes than any state in America. Aren't we lucky? Thirteen different kinds of rattlesnakes call Arizona home. The Western Diamondback is the biggest rattler in the state. It can grow up to 6 feet long. The creature is one of the most venomous snakes living in the United States. The snake's skin has a pattern of light-bordered dark diamonds and hexagonal blotches. It has a thick, heavy body and a long, black tongue. When alarmed, it rattles its tail to frighten off the intruder. Translated into human language, the sound means: "Back off dude! I am dangerous! Stay back dude…or I might bite!" ☆ A rattlesnake's rattle is nothing like a baby rattle. You knew that already. But did you know that the rattle is made of hard sections of old skin? The snake adds a new rattle each time it sheds its skin. The shedding process is called molting. Usually a shy reptile, the snake is aggressive only when cornered and provoked. Still, more people are bitten by Diamondbacks than by any other venomous snake in North America.

ARIZONA ANIMALS, PLANTS, INSECTS & ARACHNIDS

Do rattlesnakes lay eggs?

Nope. Don't be fooled by those boxes of rattler eggs for sale in souvenir shops. Rattlesnakes are one of the few types of snakes that give birth to live young. And the babies are fully equipped with fangs and venom from day one.

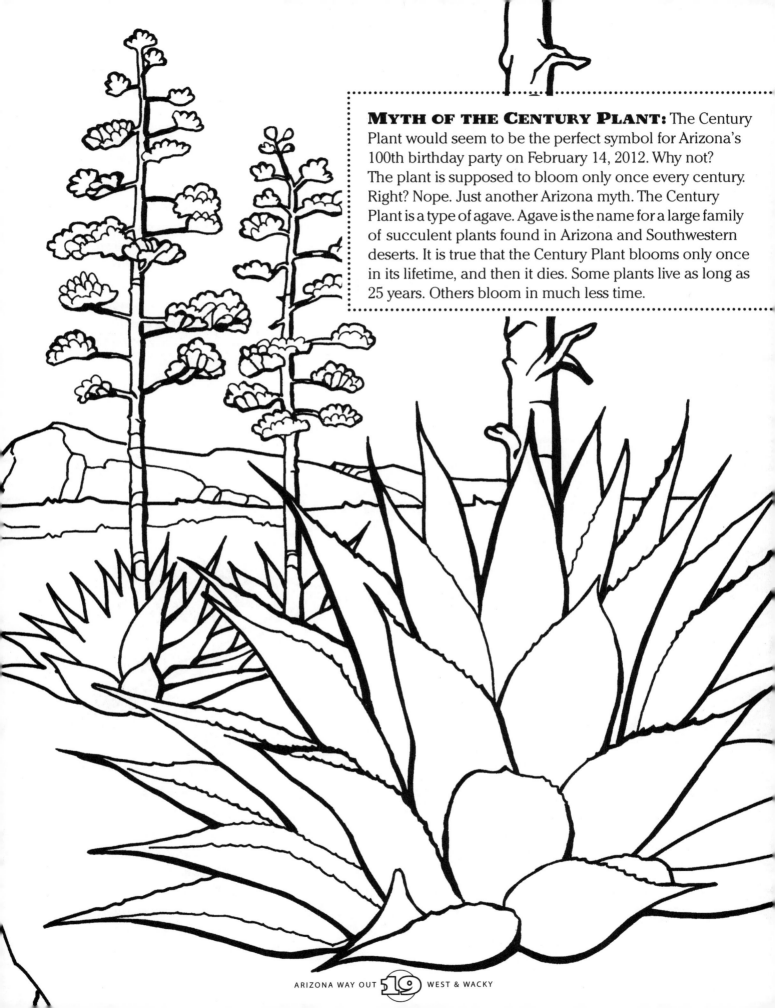

MYTH OF THE CENTURY PLANT: The Century Plant would seem to be the perfect symbol for Arizona's 100th birthday party on February 14, 2012. Why not? The plant is supposed to bloom only once every century. Right? Nope. Just another Arizona myth. The Century Plant is a type of agave. Agave is the name for a large family of succulent plants found in Arizona and Southwestern deserts. It is true that the Century Plant blooms only once in its lifetime, and then it dies. Some plants live as long as 25 years. Others bloom in much less time.

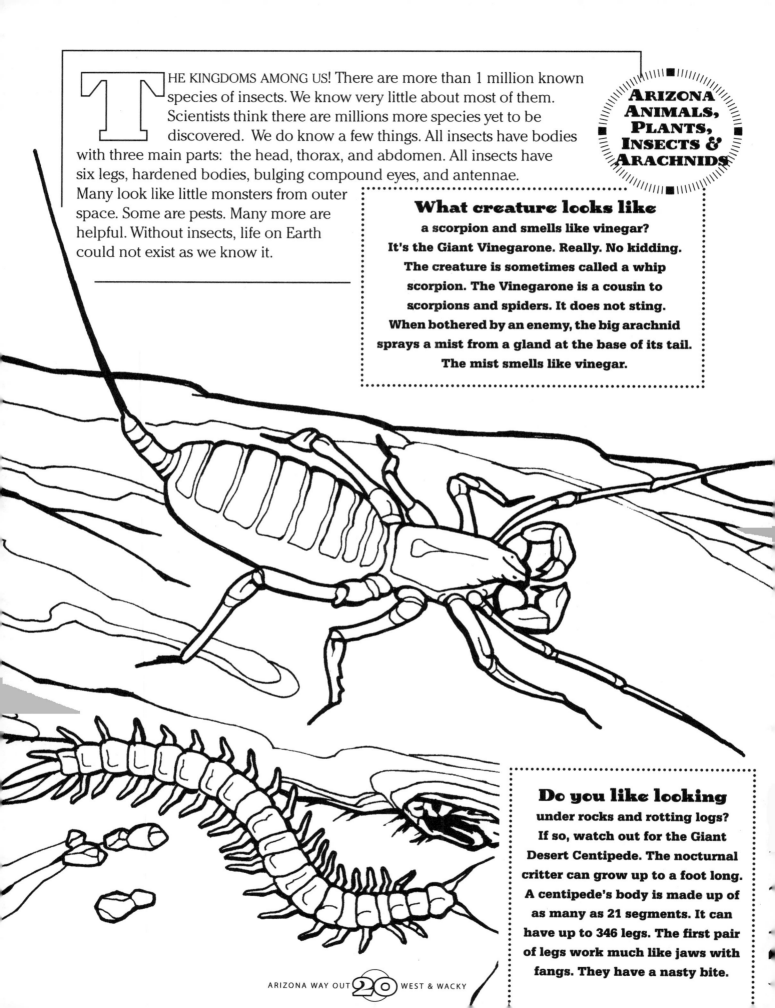

THE KINGDOMS AMONG US! There are more than 1 million known species of insects. We know very little about most of them. Scientists think there are millions more species yet to be discovered. We do know a few things. All insects have bodies with three main parts: the head, thorax, and abdomen. All insects have six legs, hardened bodies, bulging compound eyes, and antennae. Many look like little monsters from outer space. Some are pests. Many more are helpful. Without insects, life on Earth could not exist as we know it.

ARIZONA ANIMALS, PLANTS, INSECTS & ARACHNIDS

What creature looks like

a scorpion and smells like vinegar? It's the Giant Vinegarone. Really. No kidding. The creature is sometimes called a whip scorpion. The Vinegarone is a cousin to scorpions and spiders. It does not sting. When bothered by an enemy, the big arachnid sprays a mist from a gland at the base of its tail. The mist smells like vinegar.

Do you like looking

under rocks and rotting logs? If so, watch out for the Giant Desert Centipede. The nocturnal critter can grow up to a foot long. A centipede's body is made up of as many as 21 segments. It can have up to 346 legs. The first pair of legs work much like jaws with fangs. They have a nasty bite.

A lonely bee? Carpenter Bees are big. They look like fat, black bumble bees. But they live alone. That's more normal than you'd think. Only a few types of bees actually live in large groups or hives. The Carpenter Bee is named for its ability to eat through wood with strong mouthparts. It can chew a tunnel as deep as a foot into the dry wood of dead trees or houses.

Red Velvet Ants look like puffs of blazing color as they skitter across the ground. But they are not made of velvet. And they are not ants. Velvet Ants are wasps with very hairy bodies. Don't try to pick one up. The sting of a Velvet Ant is very, very painful.

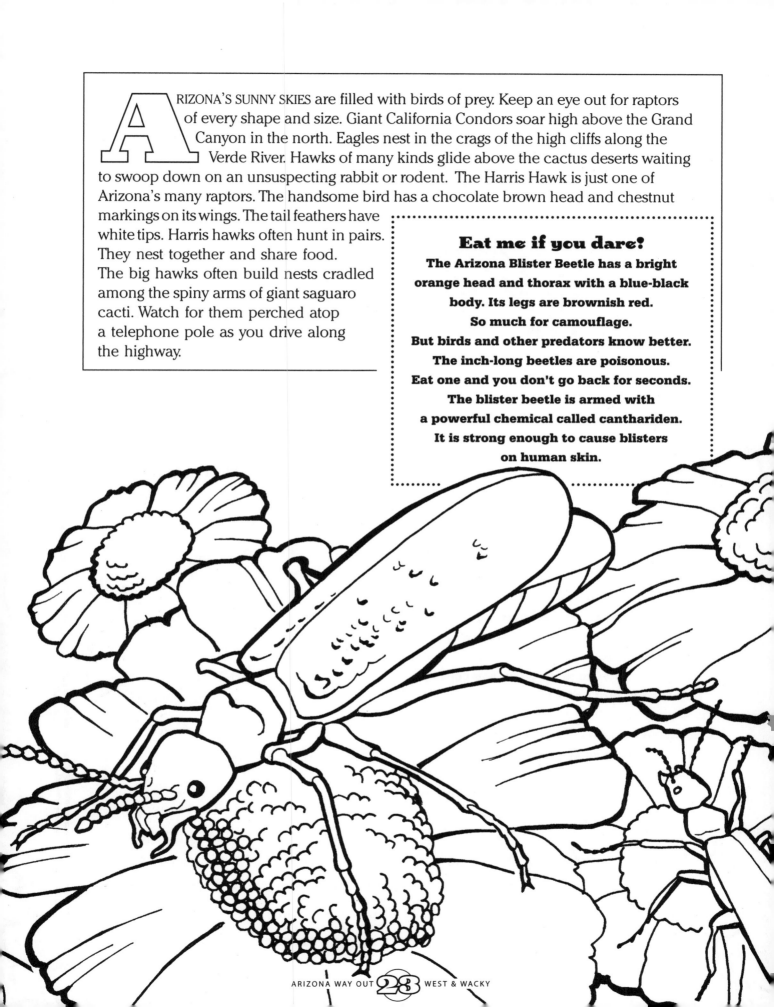

ARIZONA'S SUNNY SKIES are filled with birds of prey. Keep an eye out for raptors of every shape and size. Giant California Condors soar high above the Grand Canyon in the north. Eagles nest in the crags of the high cliffs along the Verde River. Hawks of many kinds glide above the cactus deserts waiting to swoop down on an unsuspecting rabbit or rodent. The Harris Hawk is just one of Arizona's many raptors. The handsome bird has a chocolate brown head and chestnut markings on its wings. The tail feathers have white tips. Harris hawks often hunt in pairs. They nest together and share food. The big hawks often build nests cradled among the spiny arms of giant saguaro cacti. Watch for them perched atop a telephone pole as you drive along the highway.

Eat me if you dare!
The Arizona Blister Beetle has a bright orange head and thorax with a blue-black body. Its legs are brownish red. So much for camouflage. But birds and other predators know better. The inch-long beetles are poisonous. Eat one and you don't go back for seconds. The blister beetle is armed with a powerful chemical called canthariden. It is strong enough to cause blisters on human skin.

BIG, BOLD, AND LOUD!

THE CACTUS WREN is no ordinary wren. It's not a small and shy bird, like most wrens. The Cactus Wren is big, bold, and noisy. Maybe that is why the politicians chose it to be Arizona's "Official" state bird. Measuring 7 inches to 8.5 inches from beak tip to tail tip, it's also the largest of all wrens found in the United States. ☆ The big wrens have broad white eyebrows that gleam above red eyes. Their bodies are streaked and spotted with brown and white. The top of their heads are solid brown. Cactus Wrens are not afraid to make themselves known. Listen close in the desert. Their raspy voices call out *chew, chew, chew, chew.* The birds chatter long and loud throughout the hot desert day while they hunt for insects, spiders, and lizards for lunch. ☆ Cactus Wrens build large domed nests made of weeds, grass, feathers, and twigs. They tuck the nests inside the spiny branches of cholla cactus or in the crooked arms of a giant saguaro. Bony feet and a thick coat of feathers protect them from being impaled on sharp cactus spines.

Leave me alone...

or I'll puke on you! Well, not exactly. But the turkey vulture does use vomit as a defense tactic. This is not so gross when you consider that the big bird's diet consists of road kill. Turkey vultures don't like to share their meals. If harassed by a coyote or other large predator, the bird will throw up piles of stinky chunks, and then fly away. The predator can eat the smelly mess, or not. If not, the vulture will return later to finish its nasty supper.

RED-CAPPED HOMEBUILDER

This Arizona homebuilder always wears
a red cap made of feathers. He does good work
and takes his pay in the form of bugs, worms, and
lizards. Lots of critters live in the homes he builds.
Have you seen him and his partner near your
neighborhood? Look closer. Watch for the wings
and tail with a pattern of black and white checks.
And listen. Hear the hammering sound?
Bang, bang, bang. It's the Gila Woodpecker.
☆ Every spring, male and female woodpeckers
work together. They peck holes into the thick
body of a giant saguaro cactus or into the trunks
of cottonwood trees. When the hole is deep
enough, the female builds a nest and lays three
to five small, white eggs. Deep inside the hole,
baby woodpeckers stay cool during the summer.
Elf Owls and other birds make their nests
in old woodpecker holes. Lizards and spiders
and insects of many kinds also live in the old holes.

PLANT & ANIMAL WORD SEARCH

What did one toilet say to the other?

___ ___ ___   ___ ___ ___ ___   ___ ___   ___ ___ ___   ___ ___ ___ ___ ___ ___ ___

To find the answer, complete the word search. Look for the words on the list in the grid of letters. The words can run across, up and down, diagonally, forwards or backwards! Once you've found all the words, the hidden answer will be revealed by letters that have *not* been circled. Hint: When looking for the hidden answer, start from the upper left-hand corner and look from left to right. There will be a complete sentence hidden among all the unused letters, and it will be in order.

```
T  N  S  E  V  A  E  L  Y  O  U  L  W  O  O
S  N  O  K  A  B  I  T  F  D  L  U  A  S  H
U  D  E  C  S  T  I  N  G  E  R  S  X  E  D
R  I  J  M  T  H  S  C  J  X  G  Y  Y  L  S
V  R  X  H  N  U  R  O  O  T  S  J  S  B  A
I  A  A  J  O  O  R  S  T  I  C  K  E  R  S
V  C  Z  B  I  P  R  N  H  W  U  M  N  T  O
A  N  O  Z  I  R  A  I  A  G  N  O  I  K  N
L  T  W  T  F  X  S  K  V  L  G  I  P  B  K
D  S  H  C  R  O  H  O  T  N  F  S  S  G  D
O  U  X  O  N  E  R  N  L  N  E  T  E  F  Z
J  Q  H  O  R  U  S  G  H  O  P  U  Z  P  B
T  V  R  S  F  N  I  E  I  R  E  R  C  L  M
R  A  D  V  W  Y  S  E  D  M  U  E  V  W  N
N  S  J  L  E  O  L  R  J  Q  T  P  A  D  A
```

ADAPT
ARID
ARIZONA
DESERT
DRY
ENVIRONMENT
HOT
LEAVES
MOISTURE
NOCTURNAL
ROOTS
SONORAN
SPINES
STICKERS
STINGERS
SURVIVAL
THORNS
WAXY

THEY WERE HERE FIRST!

ARIZONA OWES MUCH of its rich culture to its original dwellers. The state's Native Americans have inspired the world with handsome pottery and pretty jewelry. We enjoy their ethnic foods. We appreciate their respect for nature and spiritual folklore. And, their canals helped Phoenix thrive in the parched desert.

What is a petroglyph?

People like to draw. But they did not always have pencils, crayons, or paint. And paper is a pretty new invention. But there have always been rocks, lots of rocks. People started scratching pictures of animals and stars and other designs on rocks thousands of years ago. These pieces of rock art are called petroglyphs. What do they mean? No one knows for sure. The symbols could be related to hunting or religion. Some might be images of the sun, moon, and stars. Others might be messages left to give directions to others. More than 1,500 petroglyphs are etched onto the rocks of the Hedgepeth Hills in Phoenix. Visit the Deer Valley Rock Art Center to learn more about them.

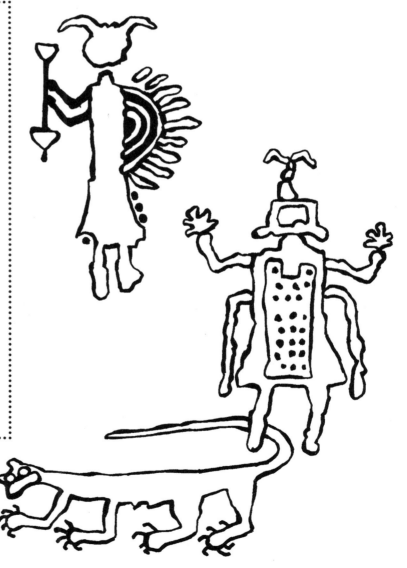

INDIGENOUS CELEBRITY

ONE OF THE COUNTRY'S celebrities came from Arizona. He was a headliner at the 1904 World's Fair in St. Louis. He rode in President Theodore Roosevelt's 1905 inaugural parade. His fans begged for his photograph. They were in awe of his memoir.   The man was Geronimo, a Chiricahua Apache.

His real name, however, was Goyathlay.   Many believe Geronimo to have been a chief. He was a fierce tribal war leader and medicine man, but never a chief. Many said he had special powers he was given during a vision. They said they saw him walk without leaving tracks. His followers said he could see the future. Some claimed he even stopped the sun from coming up to help his people escape in the dark when enemy soldiers were on their trail.   The powers came to Geronimo after he came home from a trip in 1858. He found his wife, mother, and three children murdered by Spanish troops from Mexico. He was so angry he vowed to kill as many "whites" and Mexicans as possible.

Soon after, his vision told him he would not die in battle. It said no bullet or weapon could ever kill him. It appeared to be true, too!   Geronimo was never afraid. He ignored showers of bullets during battles. He was shot many times but lived on. When he stabbed Mexican soldiers with his knife, they prayed to Saint Jerome to help them. To some it must have sounded like "Jeronimo." Soon, his enemies started calling him Geronimo.

Geronimo surrendered in 1886. But not before he and 40 warriors were able to evade 5,000 U.S. troops for more than five months. They did it without one Apache being killed or captured.

After Geronimo's surrender, the government moved him and 450 other Apaches to Florida. In 1887, Geronimo was moved to Alabama. He stayed there for seven years. Finally, he was sent to Fort Sill, Oklahoma. There he gained celebrity status. He died of pneumonia in 1909.

The girl who met Geronimo

Geronimo had a softer side. After he surrendered in 1886, the government moved him and his followers to Florida. While in transit from Arizona, his convoy made a stop at Bowie Station.

Young Addie Slaughter was among the crowd watching. Geronimo motioned to the 14-year-old girl to come closer. When she did, he took off his beaded necklace and gently placed it around her neck.

GERONIMO = GOYATHLAY SCRAMBLE

Unscramble the tiles to reveal a message. Geronimo's real name was Goyathlay.
Sometimes it was spelled Goyaalé or Goyahkla. Unscramble the word tiles
to find out what his name means in Apache.

HINT: each tile contains letters and spaces that appear in the answer phrase.
Don't rearrange letters in the tiles, keep the letters and spaces in order and unscramble the whole tiles.

Y A	E	S	WN	ON	WH	O

GHOST OF THE DRAGOONS

SOME VISITORS of the Dragoon Mountains say they have seen a man with a flute sitting on the rocks. Others say a man in Native American clothes with long black hair appeared on a hill. Could it be Cochise, the famous Chiricahua Apache chief they saw?   The area is called Cochise Stronghold. It's where Cochise holed up for 10 years as he raided his enemies. Among his foes were U.S. troops. They became his enemy when Lt. George Bascom falsely accused Cochise of kidnapping a rancher's son. Bascom told his men to arrest Cochise. When Cochise resisted, he was shot three times. Yet, he still got away by cutting his way out of a tent.   When Cochise escaped, Bascom's soldiers captured three of Cochise's family members and held them hostage. In return, Cochise attacked the Butterfield Overland stage station and snatched three employees. Bascom's army then took three more Apache prisoners. So, Cochise took three more hostages. Cochise wanted to trade his six hostages for the six Apaches. But Bascom was very stubborn and refused to return them until the rancher's son was home and safe. After a while, Cochise killed his captives. So, Bascom hung the six Apaches. The outcome was a bloody 10-year war.   In the end, Cochise surrendered twice. The first time, he went back on the run when he learned his people were going to be sent to a reservation in New Mexico in 1872. The second time he agreed to surrender when the Chiricahua Reservation was created. When he died there in 1874, his body was hidden in a secret crevice in his beloved Dragoon Mountains.

COCHISE=CHEIS SCRAMBLE

Cochise's real name was Cheis in his own language.
Unscramble the word tiles to find out what his name means.

HINT: each tile contains letters and spaces that appear in the answer phrase.
Don't rearrange letters in the tiles. Keep the letters and spaces in order and unscramble the whole tiles.

I N G H	O F	O N G T E	S T R E	H A V	A K	T H

CODE TALKERS

DURING WORLD WAR II in the Pacific, the U.S. Marines needed a secret code. They had to send messages to others without the Japanese knowing what they were saying. The Navajo language was only spoken on Navajo lands in the southwest United States. It was an unwritten language. It had no alphabet or symbols. It had its own unique tones and grammar. It was impossible to understand by anyone not trained to speak Navajo. Fewer than 30 people in the entire world who were not Navajo could speak the language during World War II. The Marines recruited Navajos in 1942. They trained them in communications. Together, they created a top secret code using the Navajo language. The brave Navajo "Code Talkers" saved many lives during the bloody battles against the Japanese. Despite their great work, the individual Code Talkers were not honored for their special service until 2001. That was more than 55 years after the war had ended. By then, only five of the 29 original Navajo Code Talkers were still alive.

The word "Navajo"
comes from a word that Spanish explorers used to refer to some native people in northeastern Arizona. The people call themselves Diné, which is usually translated as "the people of the Earth."

ARIZONA HAS 21 FEDERALLY RECOGNIZED TRIBES. **That means there are 21 tribes in the state that can receive services from the United States Bureau of Indian Affairs. They are:**

Ak Chin Indian Community of Maricopa

Cocopah Tribe of Arizona

Colorado River Indian Tribes

Fort McDowell Yavapai Nation

Fort Mojave Indian Tribe of Arizona

Gila River Indian Community

Havasupai Tribe of Havasupai Reservation

Hopi Tribe of Arizona

Hualapai Indian Tribe

Kaibab Band of Paiute Indians

Navajo Nation

Pascua Yaqui Tribe of Arizona

Quechan Tribe of Fort Yuma Indian Reservation

Salt River Pima-Maricopa Indian Community

San Carlos Apache Tribe of the San Carlos Reservation

San Juan Southern Paiute Tribe of Arizona

Tohono O'odham Nation of Arizona

Tonto Apache Tribe of Arizona

White Mountain Apache Tribe of the Fort Apache Reservation

Yavapai-Apache Nation of the Camp Verde Indian Reservation

Yavapai-Prescott Tribe of the Yavapai Reservation

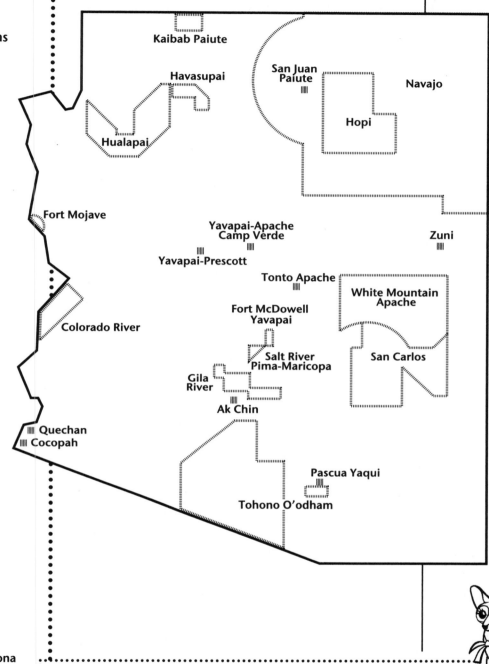

Kaibab Paiute

Havasupai

San Juan Paiute

Navajo

Hopi

Hualapai

Fort Mojave

Yavapai-Apache Camp Verde

Zuni

Yavapai-Prescott

Tonto Apache

White Mountain Apache

Colorado River

Fort McDowell Yavapai

Salt River Pima-Maricopa

San Carlos

Gila River

Ak Chin

Quechan Cocopah

Pascua Yaqui

Tohono O'odham

There are more Native American peoples living in Arizona than just the recognized 21 tribes. You may also hear of Chiricahua, Zuni, Tewa, and others that live in the state today. There are also prehistoric cultures such as the Anasazi, Hohokam, Mogollon, Patayan, and Sinagua that called the land home long before the tribes living in Arizona today. Of them, the Hohokam were Arizona's original canal builders.

FOOD FOR THOUGHT

HOW WOULD YOU LIKE TO EAT FOOD that somebody else spit out? What if instead of telling you to kill the weeds, your mom told you to pick them for dinner? ☆ The Native Peoples of Arizona "shopped" for their groceries in the wild. They had to eat what they could find or grow in Arizona's harsh climate. And, they didn't have refrigerators. To keep food from spoiling, they smoked it or dried it in the sun. ☆ Many plants didn't taste very good. People ate them anyway because nothing else could be found.

We call dandelions weeds. But, the Papago People and some early settlers thought of these plants as food. They ate the leaves raw like a salad or cooked them like spinach. Dandelions taste bitter, but they are healthy for the body.

The large, sweet fruit from the yucca plant tasted very good. To keep the fruit from spoiling, the Zuni People made yucca fruit rolls. Today, Arizona's Zunis live in the Apache County area. They also live in New Mexico on Arizona's eastern border. ☆ Zuni women picked and boiled the yucca fruit. They peeled the fruit after it cooled. That evening, all the Zuni men, women, and their neighbors had a yucca fruit chewing party. First they took the seeds out of the fruit. Then they chewed what was left. Instead of swallowing the fruit, they spit it out into a big bowl. The next day, the bowl of fruit was boiled again. When it cooled, the Zuni formed little patties with the fruit mush. Next, they put the patties on roofs to dry in the sun. They left the patties there for about three days. Finally, they put several patties together and rolled them out into long tubes. They dried the tubes a little more. At last, the tubes were ready to store or eat. These fruit tubes were really handy for traveling. That's some wacky candy! ☆ Arizona's native peoples ate all kinds of wild plants, too. They collected the beans from mesquite trees and fruit from prickly pear cacti. They dug agave roots and picked ocotillo flowers, grapes, saguaro fruits, and much more. Some Arizona tribes grew corn, beans, melons, chili peppers, and more. They also hunted for deer, rabbits, squirrels, and other animals.

FRONTIER FOODS

WHAT IF YOU WERE SICK and your dad said he knew how to make you feel better? All you had to do was eat a dead mouse and drink some tea made from sheep poop! What if you were helping mom put groceries away and she asked you to cover the eggs in animal fat before storing them? ☆ Arizona's settlers had a hard time keeping food fresh. Like Indians, they smoked and dried food. They also pickled food in vinegar and cured it in salt. They dipped hard cheeses in wax to keep them from drying out or molding. Eggs were dipped in lard and then buffed to close the pores in the eggshells. Bacteria can't get inside eggs to spoil them if the shells are sealed. The eggs were then stored in a cool place like a cellar. They could last up to six months that way. ☆ It was hard for frontier women to get yeast way out West. Often, they would make their own "starter" and use it to make bread rise. Starter is made by taking three parts whole grain flour, two parts lukewarm water, and one part sugar. The mix was put in a jar or pot with a cover and set someplace warm. By the next day, the starter would be bubbly, spongy, and kind of smelly. This meant it was fermenting. That was a good thing. ☆ Women used the starter in bread recipes like they did yeast. They had to keep feeding the starter with more sugar, flour, and water so it wouldn't die. And, they had to keep it warm. If it was too cold, they cuddled up with their jar of starter at night…instead of a Teddy bear!

☆ Prospectors and cowboys didn't want to mess with starter. They used baking powder or baking soda to make their biscuits fluffy. They cooked biscuits in a Dutch oven. A Dutch oven is a large, black iron pot with a tight lid. The entire pot got buried under the hot coals. Boy Scouts use Dutch ovens to cook with on backpacking trips. And modern men and women use them in the kitchen. ☆ What about that dead mouse and the sheep doo doo? Pioneer parents actually believed the measles could be cured by eating a roasted mouse and drinking tea made from sheep poop. Now that's wacky!

"Canning" fruits and vegetables in Mason jars was popular, and still is. A Mason jar is a glass jar with a metal lid. The lid has two pieces. One is a flat metal disk that fits snug on the top of the jar. The other is a metal ring that slips over the disk and is screwed onto the top of the jar. The Mason jar was invented in 1858. It still works well.

PIONEER DUTCH OVEN RECIPES

HEY KIDS: try your own hand at making a Dutch oven recipe just like the pioneers did! We've included a historical 1896 recipe for biscuits, a modernized Dutch oven biscuit recipe, a nationally renowned chef's recipe for "Dutch-Oven Green-Chile Cornbread," and lastly, a modern-day, easy recipe for cobbler from the Boy Scouts—made by kids your own age!

"The most enjoyable Dutch oven recipe I have ever come across is in the Flagstaff Cookbook, 1896. *It was originally compiled by the Ladies Aid Society of the Methodist Episcopal Church of Flagstaff, Arizona. We have an original in our archival collections."*

—Joe Meehan, Curator, Arizona Historical Society–Pioneer Museum

Camp Biscuit

Take a good deal of flour, more or less, according to the number of campers and the dimensions of their appetites, to which add salt "to taste" and baking powder "to raise." Mix with water into a soft dough, bake in a Dutch oven, frying pan, or whatever utensil may be at hand–using a flat stone if nothing else can be found. Serve hot on a tin plate or piece of bark, garnished with pine cones and field daisies.   —*Submitted by Frank Reid*

From the Archives of the Arizona Historical Society-Pioneer Museum, Flagstaff. Visit www.arizonahistoricalsociety.org for more information.

The recreation staff at South Mountain Park in Phoenix puts on an event called "Dutch Oven Get Your Dog On!" at which community members share favorite recipes. Mark "Dutch" Wilkins, director of the Arizona chapter of IDOS (International Dutch Oven Society), contributed this recipe. Visit www.idos.com/chapters/arizona.php for more IDOS details. Visit http://phoenix.gov/recreation/rec/parks/index.html for more about Phoenix parks.

Biscuits Made Easy

2 cups self-rising flour
1 cup heavy whipping cream
½ stick of butter, melted

Combine flour and whipping cream in a mixing bowl, stirring until just blended. Dough will be a little stiff. Transfer dough to a lightly floured surface and knead 10 times. Roll to desired thickness, about ½ inch, and cut with a 2-inch round cutter.

If using a cast iron skillet or Dutch oven, melt butter in the cast iron. Then dip cut biscuit in butter and place in cast iron buttered side up. Bake at 450 degrees for about 10 minutes or until golden brown. Makes about 12 biscuits.

Mike Mikac, a long-time leading figure with Tempe's Boy Scouts of America Troop 697, Grand Canyon Council, contributes this Scout favorite. The boys in his troop have been making it for years, and can handle everything involved from fire starting to mixing, to cooking and, of course, eating. More at www.bsatroop697.com

EZ Cobbler (10 to 12 servings)

4 16-ounce cans pie filling (apple, blueberry, cherry or peach)
2 boxes yellow or white cake mix
4 to 8 teaspoons cinnamon
1 stick butter (optional)
Cool Whip or ice cream (optional)

Start the charcoal (about 3 to 4 dozen briquettes). For easy clean-up, line a 12-inch, non-deep Dutch oven with heavy-duty aluminium foil (smooth out the sides, bottom, and along the edges where the lid seats).

Spread out the pie filling into the Dutch oven. Sprinkle unprepared cake mix over filling. Sprinkle generous amount of cinnamon powder over the cake mix. (If you choose to use the butter, slice it in ¼-inch thick pieces and scatter over the top of the cake mix before sprinkling the cinnamon powder.) Note: If you use apple filling, sprinkle cinnamon over both the pie filling and the cake mix.

Cover Dutch oven and load up a single layer of charcoal on the lid and underneath. Bake for 45 to 60 minutes (check at 30 minutes and remove some coals from the lid if the top of the cobbler is starting to darken).

When done, remove all coals, crack lid, and allow to cool for 30 minutes before dishing out. Smother with Cool Whip or ice cream if desired.

Nationally acclaimed, culinary award-winning Chef Chuck Wiley, whose roles include executive chef positions at the historic Hotel Valley Ho, Trader Vic's, Café ZuZu and Sanctuary on Camelback Mountain, contributes this Dutch oven recipe. For more information on Hotel Valley Ho, visit www.hotelvalleyho.com or call 480-248-2007.

Dutch-Oven Green-Chile Cornbread (makes 8 servings)

1 cup unsalted butter, plus extra to prepare pan
¾ cup sugar
4 eggs
½ cup roasted, seeded, and diced green chiles (may use canned)
1½ cups cream-style corn
½ cup grated Monterey Jack cheese
(may use jalapeño Jack for more spark)
1 cup all-purpose flour
1 cup yellow cornmeal
2 tablespoons baking powder
1 teaspoon salt

Heat oven to 325 degrees if cooking in the oven.
If cooking outside, light 18 charcoal briquettes or use the glowing embers from a wood fire.

Butter a 10-inch Dutch oven with a lid or a 9-inch square baking pan. In a large bowl, beat together the butter and sugar. Add the eggs, one at a time, beating well after each addition. Add the chiles, corn, and cheese, and mix well. Sift together the flour, cornmeal, baking powder, and salt; add to the egg mixture and mix until smooth.

To make cornbread in the Dutch oven: Pour batter into the prepared Dutch oven. If baking over a fire, place the Dutch oven on top of 9 of the briquettes (or glowing embers) and place the remaining 9 briquettes (or embers) on top of the lid. Don't let briquettes touch the bottom of the Dutch oven. The legs of the Dutch oven should keep it elevated ½ inch or so above the briquettes. Ideally, the Dutch oven should be placed in a pit just deep and wide enough to hold it so it's surrounded by a consistent, even heat. Bake approximately 1 hour.

If using a conventional oven, bake until a tester inserted into the center comes out clean, about 1 hour.

To make cornbread in the baking pan: Pour batter into the prepared pan and bake in oven until a tester inserted into the center comes out clean, about ½ hour. (The thinner pan will cook faster.)

DON'T CALL ME PIG! Do you like being called nasty names? I didn't think so. So have some sympathy for the Collared Peccary. Everyone wants to call the animal a pig. It's not a pig at all, even though it kind of looks like one. Thick, bristly black and gray hair covers the animal's thin, muscular body. A band of grayish-white fur runs from shoulder to shoulder. It looks a lot like a collar. In Arizona, the collared peccary is also known as a Javelina. The name comes from the Spanish word for javelin or spear. It refers to the animal's long, razor-sharp teeth. Javelinas also have tough, leathery snouts. They can eat cactus and other spiny desert plants without hurting their mouths. Javelinas live in family groups of five to 15 animals. Big males can weigh as much as 55 pounds. Be smart. Play it cool. NEVER, ever call a javelina a pig!

Grow your own shampoo?
Why not. Native people of Arizona did all
the time. They used the roots of the Soaptree
Yucca plant to make soap and shampoo.
Today, weavers still use the plant's long,
hard leaves to make strong baskets.

HUMMINGBIRDS live in the fast lane. Some species beat their wings as fast as 80 times per second. Ramsey Canyon and Miller Canyon are both located near Sierra Vista in southeastern Arizona. They are two of the best places in the entire world to see hummingbirds of many kinds.

Costa's Hummingbird is about the size of your thumb. It weighs about as much as a nickel. One third of the tiny bird's body is muscle. To get the energy they need for hovering, hummingbirds must eat half their body weight in sugar each day. If you were a hummingbird, how many candy bars would you have to eat each day just to stay alive?

MEXICAN-AMERICANS—
PART OF ARIZONA'S FOUNDATION

THE UNITED STATES is often called a melting pot of cultures. People of all colors, creeds, and nationalities dream of living in America. They come here in search of freedom and a better life for their children. The nation's strength is a product of its diversity. Arizona is like a miniature version of America. The state has a long history of ethnic diversity.

☆ More than 300 years ago, Spanish missionaries moved north from central Mexico to explore the region that today is Arizona. Soldiers came with them. So did farmers and ranchers and artists and merchants. They built churches and communities around forts called presidios. Tubac and Tucson were two of the largest. In 1853, a large chunk of what we know as southern Arizona became a part of the United States. The change happened as part of a treaty with Mexico. The deal was called The Gadsden Purchase. It added an area of land the size of Scotland to the United States. All of the Mexican residents living in the area became American citizens. These people were members of families that had lived here for generations. Many of their children moved on and helped to settle Yuma, Tempe, Florence, Casa Grande, Phoenix, and other towns across the new Arizona territory.

Making Arizona home!

An exhibit at Tempe's History Museum outlines a portion of Arizona's Hispanic heritage. During the Mexican Revolution of 1910, thousands of Mexican citizens came north to seek refuge. Between 1910 and 1930, historians say that one-tenth of the entire population of Mexico came to the United States. Tens of thousands of those people went to work and made homes in Arizona. Like the English and German and Irish and Chinese and Swedish and Italian and other settlers before them, they became Americans.
That's not wacky...that's inspiring!

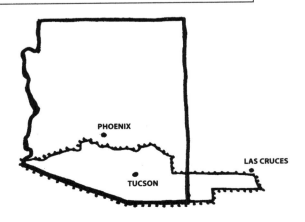

Proud of their heritage

Arizona is home to many famous Mexican-Americans. The list of their names and accomplishments is huge. Visit your local library or museum to learn more about them. But we thought you should know at least a bit about Cesar Chavez and Placida Garcia Smith.

Cesar Estrada Chavez (1927-1993) was born in 1927 on his family's farm near Yuma, Arizona. He and his family became migrant farm workers when they lost the farm during the Great Depression. They followed the seasons across the Southwest, working in fields and vineyards picking vegetables and fruit. Young Cesar learned the hardships and injustices of life as a farm worker. Lessons learned during those tough times bore amazing fruit of their own. ☆ Chavez's dream was to create an organization to protect and serve farm workers. In 1962, he helped to found the National Farm Workers Association. That group became the United Farm Workers of America, the first successful farm workers union in American history. Chavez led the UFWA for more than three decades, always fighting for the rights of migrant farm workers everywhere. ☆ Senator Robert F. Kennedy called Cesar Chavez "one of the heroic figures of our time." The impact he made is still felt today in the phrase, "Si se puede." It means, "Yes we can." ☆ In 1993, his family and friends established the Cesar E. Chavez Foundation. The goal is to educate people about the life and work of this important American civil rights leader. The hope is to inspire young people to carry on his values and vision for a better world.

Placida Garcia Smith (1896-1981) was born in Conejos, Colorado. But it was in Arizona that she earned her reputation as a true patriot. She spent her life teaching, sharing, and caring for others. As director of Friendly House in downtown Phoenix, she helped more than 1,400 people become American citizens. ☆ Garcia Smith moved to Phoenix in 1928 when her husband, Reginald, took a job with what is today Phoenix Newspapers, Inc. Placida went to work as a substitute teacher at Phoenix Elementary School. She had worked as a teacher and school principal for years in Colorado. In 1931, she began what would become a 30-plus year career as the director of Friendly House.
☆ Friendly House was set up as a center to help immigrants learn the ways of their adopted country. Men found help to get jobs. Woman learned American housekeeping skills. Many got jobs working as maids and cooks. Everyone learned English and what it meant to be an American citizen. ☆ Placida Garcia Smith is a member of the Arizona Women's Hall of Fame. In his nomination letter, U.S. District County Judge Valdemar A. Cordova wrote about her passion for her students. He wrote, "In helping them attain their goal... she instilled in them an understanding that freedom to be an American is more than merely a word. It is a spirit and a way of life."

HISPANIC HERITAGE RECIPES

Try your hand at making some of the yummy recipes that stemmed from Arizona's Hispanic heritage!

Recipes contributed by Roni Capin Rivera-Ashford, a native Arizonan who has lived in the Sonoran Desert region of Arizona since infancy. She is also the author of My Nana's Remedies/ Los Remedios de mi Nana, *which took first place in the "Cultural Diversity" and "Family Matters" categories in the acclaimed Purple Dragonfly Book Awards. The contest honors exceptional children's books. Visit www.PurpleDragonflyBookAwards.com and click on Bookstore for more info.*

Tostadas

4 tostada shells
1 can refried beans, or 2 cups whole, cooked pinto beans mashed (heat before using)
2 cups each, chopped: lettuce, tomatoes, radishes, green onions
1 cup shredded longhorn or Jack cheese, or queso fresco, or Cotija cheese
1 cup chopped black olives (optional)
1 to 2 cups shredded chicken or cooked chorizo (optional)
salsa

Spread refried beans on tostada shell with back of a spoon. Sprinkle vegetables (and olives, if selected) in layers on top of beans. Sprinkle chicken or chorizo on top of veggies (if meat is desired). Sprinkle cheese on top of meat or vegetables. Top with your favorite salsa, or none. Don't worry about being messy. Have lots of napkins handy and enjoy. Serves 4.

Cheese or Chicken Enchiladas

1 12-count package of corn tortillas
1 32-ounce can of Las Palmas Enchilada Sauce
canola oil
1 pound of shredded Jack cheese
shredded lettuce
chopped black olives and radishes
shredded chicken (optional)
sour cream (optional)

Warm to soften corn tortillas in hot oil in pan on stove. Dip 1 warmed tortilla in bowl of enchilada sauce. Place tortilla covered with sauce in baking pan. Put shredded cheese in middle of tortilla (and chicken, if selected). Roll up tortilla with ingredients in the middle. Repeat this process until all 12 enchiladas are rolled in pan. Bake in oven, heated to 350 degrees, for 12 to 15 minutes. Remove from oven and place enchiladas on plates using a spatula. Sprinkle lettuce, radish, and chopped olives on top of enchiladas. Add sour cream on top, if you'd like. Serves 6.

Salsa

1 16-ounce can diced tomatoes (or use 3 to 4 fresh depending on size)
1 4-ounce can diced green chilies (or 2 to 3 fresh serrano or jalapeño peppers)
2 cloves fresh garlic (diced or minced) or 1 teaspoon minced garlic (from a jar)
½ teaspoon salt
¼ teaspoon pepper
½ teaspoon dried oregano
¼ teaspoon dried cumin powder (optional)
3 green onions, chopped fine
½ cup fresh cilantro, chopped fine
1 diced avocado (optional)

Mix all ingredients together. Refrigerate when not using. Serves 4 to 6.

Arroz Con Leche (Rice Pudding)

1 cup white rice
2 cups water
2 cinnamon sticks, or 1 teaspoon ground cinnamon
1 pinch salt
4 cups milk (for richer pudding substitute 1 can evaporated milk,
and add regular milk to equal 4 cups)
1 egg
1 cup sugar (to taste)
1 teaspoon vanilla extract
1 tablespoon very fine julienne strips lime peel (optional)
⅓ cup raisins (optional)

Place the rice in a large saucepan with the water, cinnamon sticks, lime peel, and salt.
Bring to a boil; lower the heat and cook, covered, until most of the water has been absorbed.
Beat the egg. Add egg to milk. Add milk-egg mixture and sugar to cooked rice, stirring
constantly over low heat until the mixture thickens. Add vanilla and raisins (if using) and
cook for 2 minutes. Remove from the heat and let cool for 10 to 20 minutes. Transfer to
a loaf pan or individual bowls and refrigerate. Garnish with ground cinnamon if desired.
Serves 6 to 8. For more fun, listen to the song "Arroz Con Leche" sung by José Luis Orozco.

Fruit Salsa

1 large mango, peeled and diced –or– ¼ peeled and diced pineapple
1 fresh jalapeño pepper, diced and seeded
¼ cup chopped cilantro
1 green onion, finely chopped
¼ teaspoon salt
Juice from 1 key lime
1 tablespoon olive oil

Mix all together. Refrigerate when not using. Serves 2 to 4.

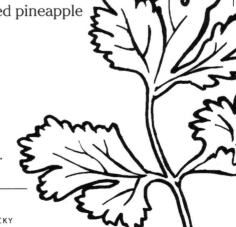

HOME SWEET HOME

YOU'D PROBABLY THINK it was pretty wacky if you discovered your classmates kept their underwear in the freezer! Or slept in wet sheets! Doing that stuff was actually pretty smart if you lived in the Arizona desert a long time ago. Willis Carrier invented air conditioning in 1902. But it wasn't easy to get AC for homes until after World War II. People actually chilled their clothes to stay cool. They hung wet sheets in doorways and windows. The air cooled as it blew through sheets. Some families slept on the floor or on big porches at night. It was cooler than sleeping in beds. Covered porches were also useful during the day. They kept the hot sun from shining in the windows and heating up the house. Big shade trees kept houses cooler, too. Air conditioning made living in Arizona much more comfy. After AC arrived, many more people moved to the state. This meant more houses needed to be built. Builders liked that. But it wasn't Arizona's first housing boom. Before 1887, most buildings in Phoenix were made of adobe bricks. Adobe is made from sun-dried clay and straw. Builders didn't use wood because it cost a lot of money. Wood had to be shipped a long distance by wagons. That was expensive. And wagons were slow, so it took longer to get wood from one place to another. In 1887, Phoenix got connected with the railroad. Lumber could be sent by train, which made it cheaper. Trains were also faster. This led to a building boom. Wood-framed houses in the desert were cheaper to build than adobe. But they were not cooler. Progress can be a funny thing.

**Montezuma Castle
National Monument** is located
in the Verde Valley. The first miners and
U.S. soldiers visited the area in the 1860s and
misnamed it after the Aztec emperor, Montezuma.
In fact, the massive dwelling was built by Arizona
native Sinagua people nearly 1,000 years ago.

KEEPING COOL IN THE DESERT

What kind of cheese is not yours?

When you unscramble the words below, they will all spell something that can help keep you or your house cool in the hot Arizona summer. Unscramble the words and spell out the correct word with the letters in the boxes. Some answers are two words. Some boxes are shaded. Each shaded box will contain a letter that will help you solve the answer to the riddle. Once you have all the letters from the shaded boxes written down, unscramble them, and you will have the answer.

I E C

N O D I N T E R C R O I I A

E T A R W

O L P O

P L P I C S E O

A H D S E

R I S T E M

F N A

S T H W S E T E E

R W P A O O C L E S M

JUST FOR FUN

ARIZONA CHILDREN'S PLAYTHINGS & PASTIMES

APPLES, CORNHUSKS, HOOPS, AND STICKS were all part of the toys Arizona boys and girls played with long ago. Pioneer girls kissed apples goodnight. They also hugged cornhusks as they slept. That's because parents used apples and cornhusks to make dolls for their children. Most people couldn't afford to buy fancy dolls. They used whatever materials they had laying around. Apples were used for doll heads. They were peeled, dried, and carved for faces. Cornhusks were soaked in water to soften. Then they were tied together with twine to form heads and bodies. Cornhusks were also used for arms and legs. ☆ Hoop rolling was another way to have fun. Kids looked for wooden hoops about the size of a bicycle tire. They pushed the hoops with a wooden stick. Kids competed to see who could keep the hoops rolling the longest. They also raced each other from place to place. ☆ Spinning tops were made of round wooden disks. Each disk had a hole cut in the middle. A dowel or peg was snugly pushed through the hole. Children picked up the top by the peg using their thumb and middle finger. Still holding the top, they placed it on the floor or table on the bottom peg. Then they would move their thumb and middle finger fast, as if they were snapping their fingers. This made the top spin. Some people think that acorns were the first tops. ☆ Marbles, pickup sticks, jump rope, yo-yos, and jacks were other fun games played by Arizona kids. But if you think the board game was a modern invention, think again. The Hopi people of Arizona played a game called Tuknanavuhpi. The game was played on a stone slab. A pattern etched on the stone looked much like a checkerboard. The Hopi also used game pieces that were similar to checkers. King me!

The object of the game is to capture all of an opponents' pieces. The player who does so wins. The game is played very much like checkers. For complete rules, visit http://en.wikipedia.org/wiki/tuknanazuhpi

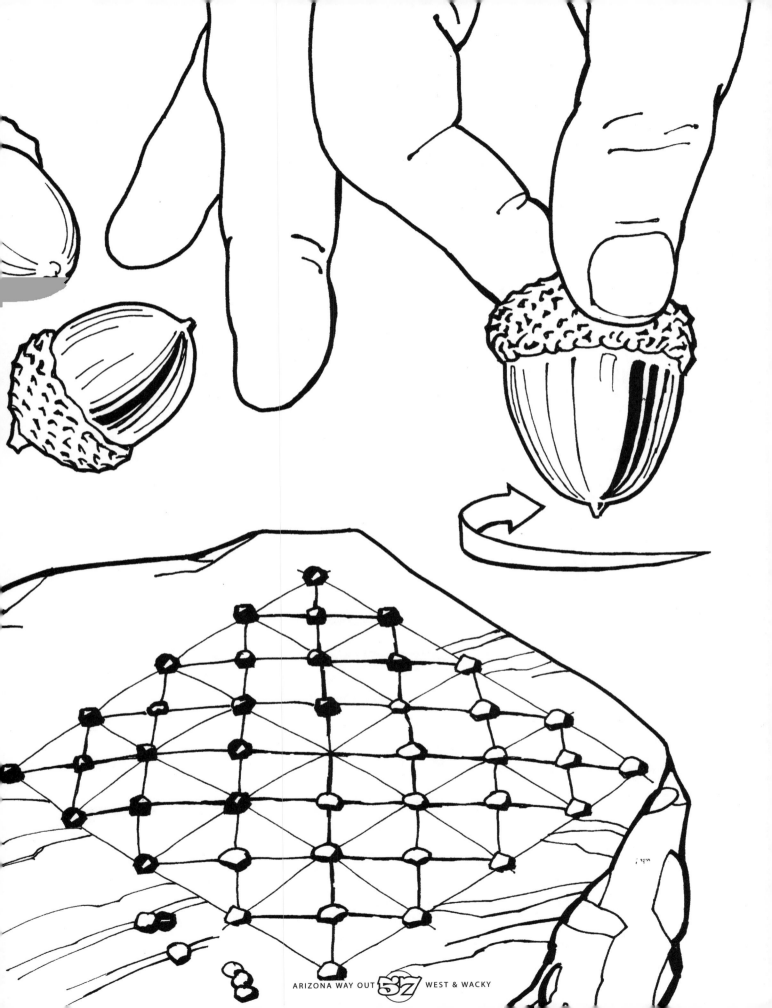

MAKE A CORNHUSK DOLL

MATERIALS NEEDED: String or yarn, scissors, a bucket of water (preferably warm), bags of cornhusks (dried, cleaned and in uniform sizes–most easily purchased at a local craft or grocery store).

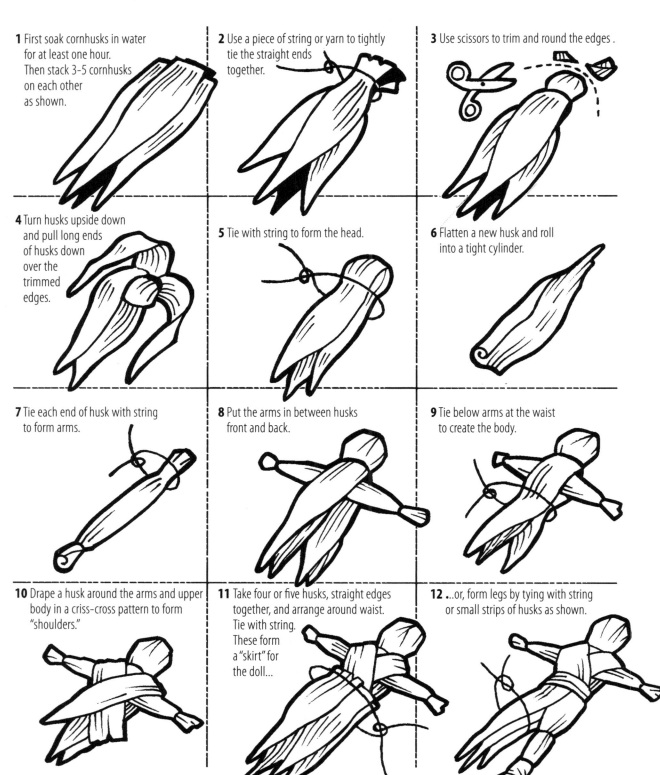

1 First soak cornhusks in water for at least one hour. Then stack 3-5 cornhusks on each other as shown.

2 Use a piece of string or yarn to tightly tie the straight ends together.

3 Use scissors to trim and round the edges .

4 Turn husks upside down and pull long ends of husks down over the trimmed edges.

5 Tie with string to form the head.

6 Flatten a new husk and roll into a tight cylinder.

7 Tie each end of husk with string to form arms.

8 Put the arms in between husks front and back.

9 Tie below arms at the waist to create the body.

10 Drape a husk around the arms and upper body in a criss-cross pattern to form "shoulders."

11 Take four or five husks, straight edges together, and arrange around waist. Tie with string. These form a "skirt" for the doll...

12 ...or, form legs by tying with string or small strips of husks as shown.

Finish off the doll by tying small strips of husk around the neck and waist to hide the string. Small scraps of cloth may be used to dress the doll, to create hair, or other decoration.

This fun craft was contributed by the Rosson House Museum. Visit www.RossonHouseMuseum.org to learn more.

SMALLEST OWL COULD BE SANTA'S HELPER: What is the smallest owl living in Arizona? Here's a hint: Who helps make all the toys for Santa Claus? Elves, of course. And the smallest owl of all is the Elf Owl. The tiny bird is only 5 to 6 inches tall from the top of its head to the tip of its tail. That's about as long as a brand new pencil.

☆ The Elf Owl is no chicken. It uses its sharp beak and talons to kill and eat scorpions. Crickets, beetles and insects of many kinds also make tasty treats. They can snatch moths and mosquitoes from the air while flying.

☆ The little owls lay eggs the size of jelly beans. They make their nests in abandoned woodpecker holes. Elf owls have bright yellow eyes with white eyebrows. Look close when hiking in the desert. You might see those eyes watching you from a hole in the trunk of a giant saguaro cactus.

At 5 years of age, a Saguaro Cactus is only about 6 inches tall. The giant cactus begins life as a tiny, black seed inside a bright red fruit. Each fruit holds thousands of seeds the size of a pinhead. Only one of every 500,000 seeds will become a fully grown cactus.

DESERT GIANTS

The Saguaro Cactus is the biggest cactus of them all. But it only grows in the Sonoran Desert of Arizona and northern Mexico. The massive plant can live for 200 years. The giant cactus is like a living desert hotel. All kinds of birds, animals, insects, and reptiles live in and around the Saguaro. A full-grown Saguaro can stand more than 50 feet tall and weigh more than 8 tons. That's as much as five cars. The Saguaro Cactus has a woody skeleton. The "ribs" expand like an accordion to store water in the plant's trunk and many spiny arms. A full-grown Saguaro can hold enough water to fill 1,000 bathtubs.

ARIZONA IS HOME to many different kinds of bats. Many of the flying mammals prefer the bug buffet. A hungry little brown bat can gobble as many as 1,000 mosquitoes per hour. Other types can eat their body weight in bugs every night.

The Nightblooming Cereus
is sometimes called the
Arizona Queen of the Night. The plant's
flower blooms and stays open for only
one night. You can smell a Cereus flower
from more than 100 feet away.

WHAT'S IN A NAME?

MANY ARIZONA CITIES are named after people. Some are named for plants or events. Others are named with Spanish or Native American words. However, some cities actually got their names by mistake. One was even named as a result of a poker game.

☆ Take the town of Rye, for example. Rye is a small town just south of Payson. The town got its name because the first settlers there noticed the creek's banks were covered with wild rye. Cottonwood was named for a grove of old cottonwood trees that grows there. What about Cornville? Do you think it was named because of all the corn growing there? Wrong! The town was supposed to be called Cohnville after a family named Cohn. The paperwork was sent to Washington D.C. to make Cohnville the official name. When the paperwork came back, however, it read Cornville. Let that be a lesson for good penmanship!

Show Low had the wackiest way of all to get its name. The town is located in the White Mountains of northeastern Arizona. Two men named C.E. Cooley and Marion Clark lived on a 100,000-acre settlement there. Legend says that the men decided the town just wasn't big enough for both of them. They agreed to play a game of poker. The loser would have to move out. The story goes that Clark said, "If you show low, you win." Cooley drew a Two of Clubs, the lowest card of all. He said, "Show Low it is."

☆ Watch for the sign that says Horsethief Basin when your family travels on Interstate-17 between Phoenix and Flagstaff. The area was a hideout for outlaws and their stolen horses.

Flagstaff has its own name roots in a tall pine tree. In 1876, a group of settlers from Boston cut the branches off the tree. They used the log as a pole to raise the American flag. Staff is another word for pole. So the town was called Flagstaff. Guess Flagstaff just sounds a lot better than Flagpole. Don't you agree? ☆ The earliest community in the Phoenix area was called Swillings. Later, it was called Helling Mill, after the owner of the town's flour mill. Eventually, a committee was formed to select an official name. Darrell Duppa was part of that group. He suggested the name Phoenix, like the mythical bird that rose out of its ashes. The new city of Phoenix was built upon the ruins of the ancient Hohokam civilization. The name was accepted. However, there is another theory. Old military maps show the name spelled Phenix rather than Phoenix. This led some to conclude that the city was named after John Derby, an army officer and writer. Derby's pen name was John Phenix.

ARIZONA NAME GAME

Race your friends or classmates to see who can get from
Nogales to the Grand Canyon by answering each Arizona city riddle.

Begin at "START." When you correctly answer question 1, you advance to point 1 on the map—mark or circle number 1. Then when you correctly answer question 2, you advance to point 2, so mark off number 2. When you answer riddle 10, you have made it to the Grand Canyon!

Name an Arizona city that....

1...would go with you to your grave

☐☐☐☐☐☐☐☐☐☐

2... you would find in a book

☐☐☐☐

3... came from Florida

☐☐☐☐☐☐☐

4...is better than all the others

☐☐☐☐☐☐☐☐☐☐

5... that has no worries

☐☐☐☐☐☐☐☐☐

6... is as big as the world

☐☐☐☐☐☐

7...would live in a castle

☐☐☐☐☐☐☐☐

8...would fall from the sky

☐☐☐☐☐☐☐☐☐☐☐

9... is something you would never expect

☐☐☐☐☐☐☐☐☐

10...would get you wet in the morning

☐☐☐☐☐☐

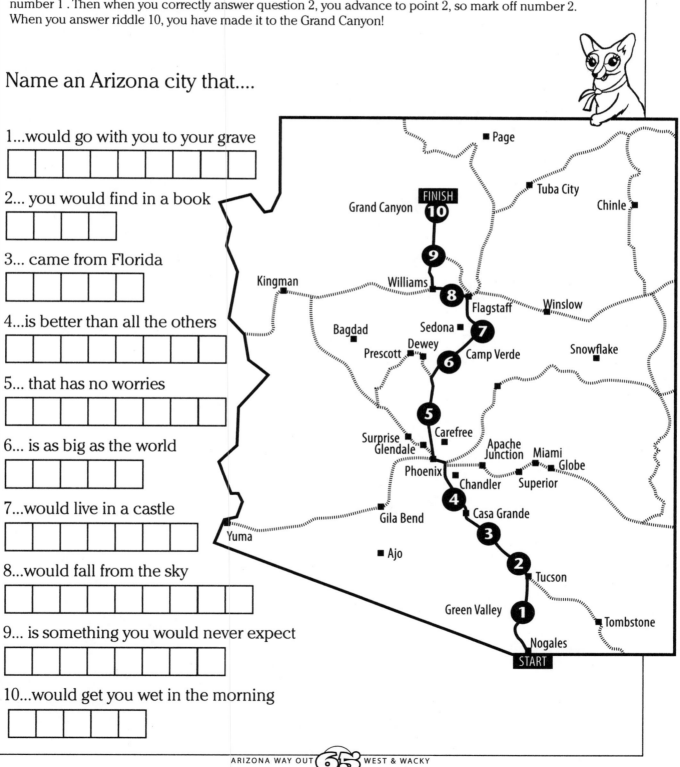

Why does the Jackrabbit

have long ears? To stay cool in the desert, of course. The animal's foot-long ears help control its body temperature. During hot days, the long ears stand straight up. Inside each ear's thin skin, a network of blood vessels gives off heat, cooling the Jackrabbit's body.

The Antelope Jackrabbit

is actually a hare, not a rabbit at all. The animal can run in speedy bursts up to 50 miles per hour. Such speed is handy when being chased by a coyote. But jackrabbits need to keep an eye on the sky at all times. Running speed is no match for a swooping hawk.

OLD MAN OF THE DESERT: The Mohave, Great Basin, and Sonoran deserts cover large chunks of Arizona from north to south. Plants and animals living in those deserts have to be tough. The Desert Tortoise is one of those creatures. It can live for 80 years or more. The tortoise is no speedster. It does not run from predators. Head, legs, and tail fit snugly inside the safety of its hard shell when danger is near. The shell also provides shade from the blistering desert sun.   The tortoise has sharp, serrated jaws that look a lot like a bread knife. The jaws are perfect for shredding tough grass and thick, pulpy cactus pads and blossoms. The tortoise gets some moisture from the food it eats. It takes long drinks whenever water is available.

But the creature also saves up for the hot, dry days ahead. The tortoise can store a month's supply of water in a special sac under its shell. It's a true desert survivor.

The Fishhook Barrel Cactus
is sometimes called the "Water Barrel."
It holds moisture long after other desert plants are withered and dry. Curved red spines protect the plant's body. Native Americans used the sharp spines as fishhooks.

GHOSTS OF
HISTORY PAST

IF YOU ARE VISITING The Old Dominion Mine in the Miami-Globe area, and you hear a knocking sound, you might want to run away…fast! It could be Tommyknockers warning you of danger. At least that's what some miners in the area believed. Tommy-knockers were thought to be little gnomes who lived in the cracks and faults of mines. The miners believed the souls of dead miners lived inside the little creatures. It is said they knocked on mine walls and threw stones at miners to warn them of a cave-in. However, the knocking was more likely just the creaking sounds of the mine's timbers. The Old Dominion Mine closed in 1931. However, not before it produced a lot of copper ore. Visit the Gila County Historical Museum to learn more about the area. It's housed in what was the old Globe-Miami Mine Rescue Station.

You can visit the Vulture Mine and walk around the town. The Assay Office is made with low-grade ore. Some say it contains $6,000 worth of silver and gold in its walls. You can also see a blacksmith shop, bunkhouses, mess hall, mill, and two old schoolhouses. But, if you see a ghostly figure lurking around, you will never know for sure who it is. It could be the spirit of a dead miner, a thief who was hung, or old Henry Wickenburg himself. Then again, it might just be the desert sun in your eyes.

FOR A CLOSE LOOK at a true ghost town, visit the Vulture Mine in Wickenburg. The town is named after Henry Wickenburg. He found gold ore in the area. But instead of mining it himself, he sold the ore still in the ground for $15 a ton. The buyers had to mine the ore, move it out, and mill it themselves. It seemed like a good idea at the time. That was before the miners began to pocket the ore. During the first six years Vulture Mine was open, workers stole 40 percent of the mine's gold! Some of the miners were caught, and hung on the "hanging tree." In 1923, more miners died when they chipped ore out of a rock wall that was supporting the Vulture mine. The mine collapsed. The cave-in buried seven miners and 12 donkeys. ☆ Vulture mine was the richest mine in Arizona during the 19th century. But Henry Wickenburg didn't die happy or as a rich man. He sold almost half his interest in the mine to Ben Phelps. But Phelps never paid him the money. In 1905, Wickenburg committed suicide. The mine closed in 1942.

GOLD, GREED, AND MINING TOWNS

ACROSS

1 It was often the penalty for stealing from a mine.
3 This "Old" mine was located in Miami-Globe.
5 The first name of the man after whom the town of Wickenburg was named.
6 What percent of the ore was stolen from the Vulture mine?
8 A danger faced by miners.
10 They were believed to contain the dead souls of miners.
11 The name of a famous mine in Wickenburg.

DOWN

2 The Vulture Mine building that contains $6,000-worth of silver and gold.
4 Miners take it out of the ground.
7 These support mines and help keep them from collapsing.
9 The types of valuable metal found in Arizona's mines were silver, gold, and what?

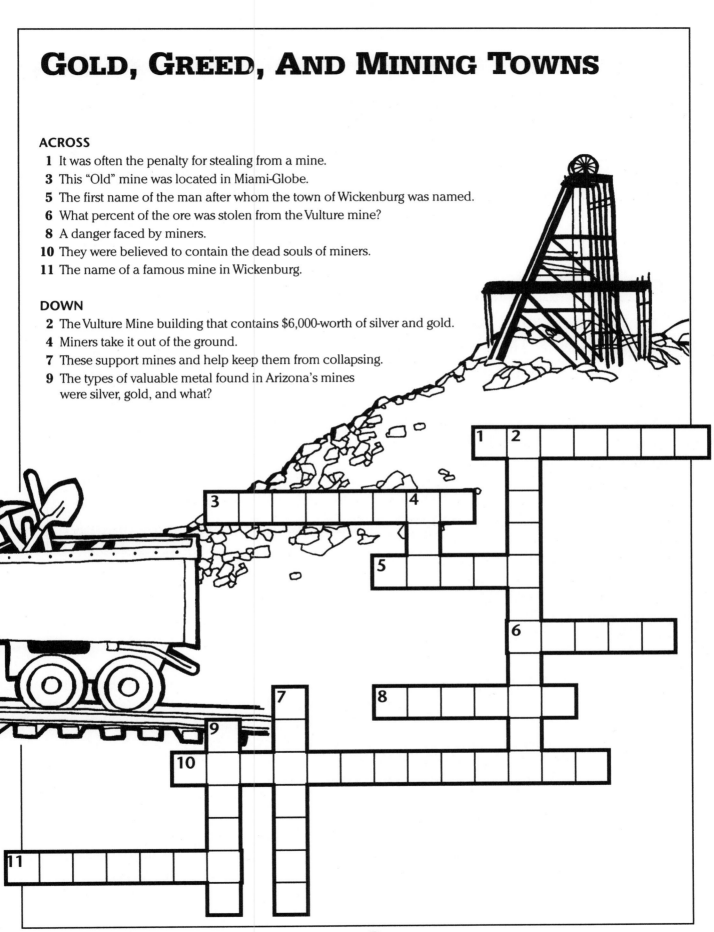

THE LEGAL FRONTIER

DO A GOOGLE SEARCH on "weird laws" in Arizona and you will see some crazy claims. Did you know it's against the law to keep a donkey in a bathtub? And, it is illegal to hunt camels in Arizona–NOT! These are myths that refuse to go away. Like rumors, they were repeated so many times people now believe they are true. If you check Arizona Revised Statutes, you will see there are no such laws. ☆ However, there is a wacky 1925 law that allowed a deck of cards determine who won a city council election in Cave Creek. The law says that an election tie can be broken "by lot." That means a game of chance. In 2009, Adam Trenk and Thomas McGuire tied for an open city council seat. The law said they could decide the winner by drawing cards. Trenk drew a King of Hearts. McGuire picked the Six of Hearts. The rest, as they say, is history.

When it comes to law breakers,

Arizona has some interesting tales. Legend has it that from the years 1863 to 1890, convicts in the town of Wickenburg were chained to a thick, old mesquite called the "Jail Tree." The 200-year-old tree still exists. The story says prisoners had to stay chained to the tree until they finished their sentence or died. Of course, that is wacky...and not true. Wickenburg had no jail. Convicts were chained to the tree until Phoenix lawmen could pick them up. In 1890, Wickenburg got a real jail.

IN 1876, the first inmates were locked in Yuma's Territorial Prison. It was a jail they built themselves! The rules were very strict. If they littered or failed to bathe, they could be forced to wear a ball and chain. Some offenders were sent to the "dark cell." It was built mostly underground. The cells were only 10 feet by 10 feet. The only light that came into the cell was from an air shaft in the ceiling. Dark cell prisoners were stripped down to their underwear. They were only given bread and water once a day. The convicts had another name for the dark cell. They called it the "snake den." ☆ In 1908, the Arizona State Prison Complex at Florence was planned. Inmates lived in tents while they built the prison with their own hands. The Florence prison is still the place where Arizona locks up some of its most notorious criminals. More than 80 inmates have been executed there by hanging, the gas chamber, or by lethal injection. The prison was first built to punish criminals with hard labor. Today, it tries to educate and rehabilitate inmates so they don't return.

JAIL TREE MAZE

You are a Phoenix lawman who has just unchained a convict from Wickenburg's Jail Tree. Can you get the prisoner out of the maze to the City of Phoenix before he escapes?

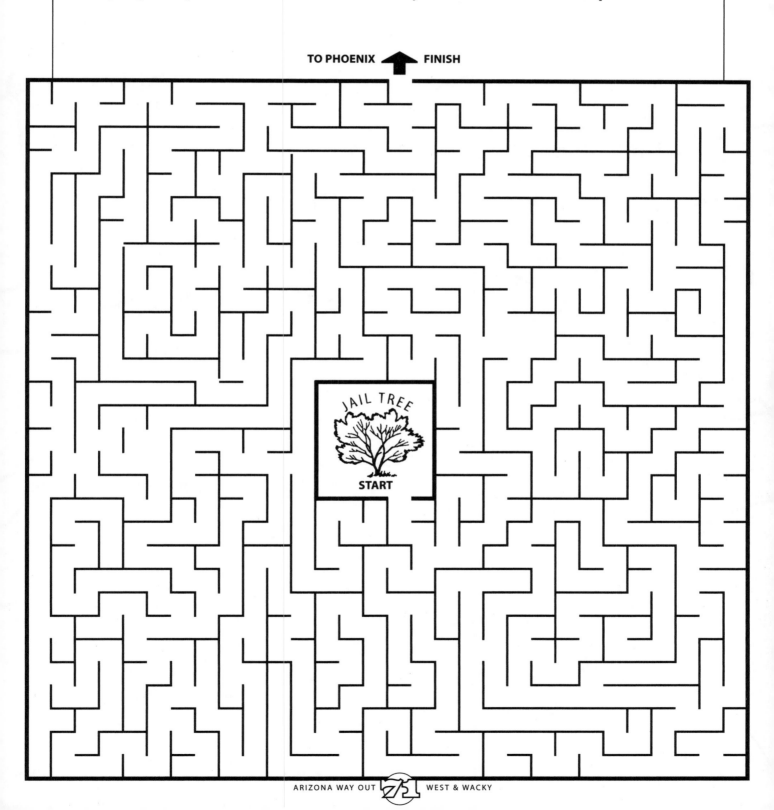

TO PHOENIX ↑ FINISH

JAIL TREE

START

RESPECT THIS MONSTER

THE GILA MONSTER is the largest lizard in Arizona. It can grow up to 2 feet long and weigh almost 5 pounds. Gila Monsters are the only venomous lizards found in the United States. The big lizards sport a mouthful of dagger-like teeth that can deliver a powerful, painful bite. ☆ Gila Monsters appear dressed for Halloween. They are covered with round scales that look like tiny beads. Their thick bodies are colored with stripes or blotches of black and shades of orange or yellow. ☆ Despite a fierce reputation, Gila Monsters are actually quite shy. They spend large portions of their life underground living in burrows stolen from rodents. When they do come out, it's usually time to feast. Gila Monsters eat mice, rats, and baby birds. Eggs are their favorite food. They gobble the eggs of birds, tortoises, snakes, and lizards. ☆ A hungry Gila Monster can eat up to one third of its weight in a single meal. To match that feat, a 60-pound third-grader would have to chow down on 80 quarter-pound burgers for supper.

Arizona cowboys and prospectors had lots of tall tales about Gila Monsters. Probably because it was rare to actually see one of the big lizards. One story says that if a Gila Monster walks through your camp at night, its breath is so bad that it can kill a cowboy asleep in his bedroll. Another story says that if a Gila Monster bit you, it would not let go until the sun goes down.

THE TARANTULA is a creature of bad dreams. The big spiders often star in Hollywood horror movies. Halloween decorations often include creepy versions of the huge, hairy eight-leggers. But don't be afraid. Tarantulas are actually shy, gentle creatures. Most Arizona tarantulas are brown or black. Some have a blonde color. One of the most beautiful is the Mexican Redknee Tarantula. It is velvet black with legs that sport bright patches of reddish-orange. One thing to remember—don't bother them and they won't bother you.

Big wimps? Tarantulas have large, sharp fangs that can deliver a dose of strong venom. But most would rather hide in a snug burrow dug into desert soil. Some tarantulas use their body hairs like tiny poison darts. When threatened by a predator, the spider rubs its body with a back leg. Clouds of tiny hairs fly into the air. The stinging hairs irritate the eyes and nose of enemies. The spider has time to run away.

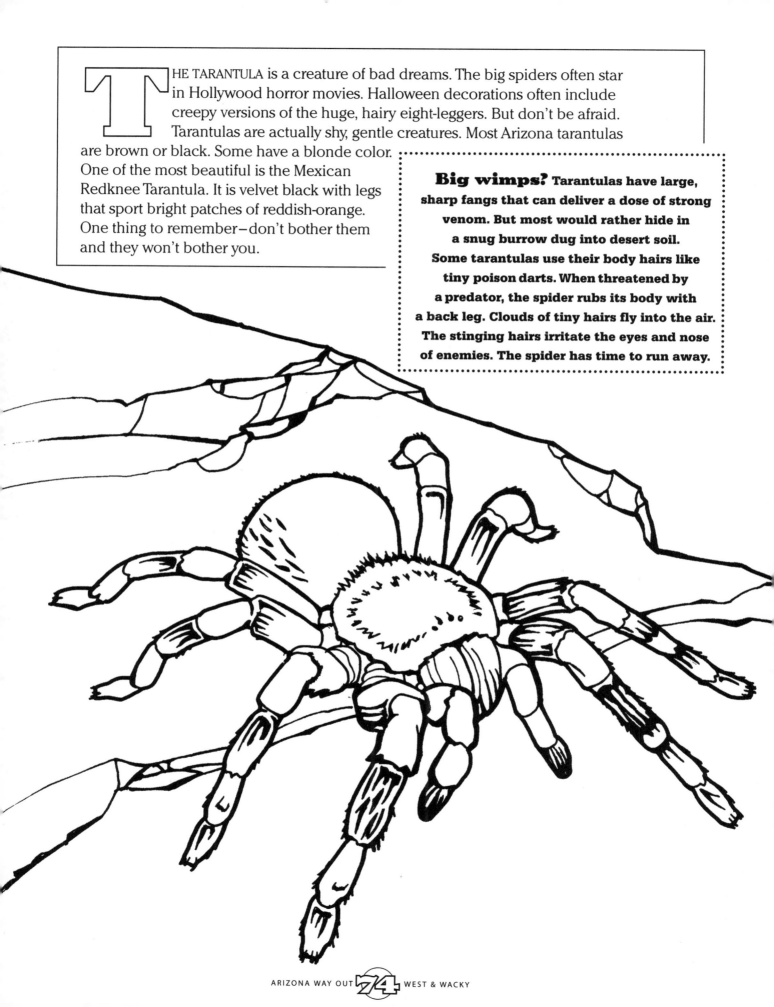

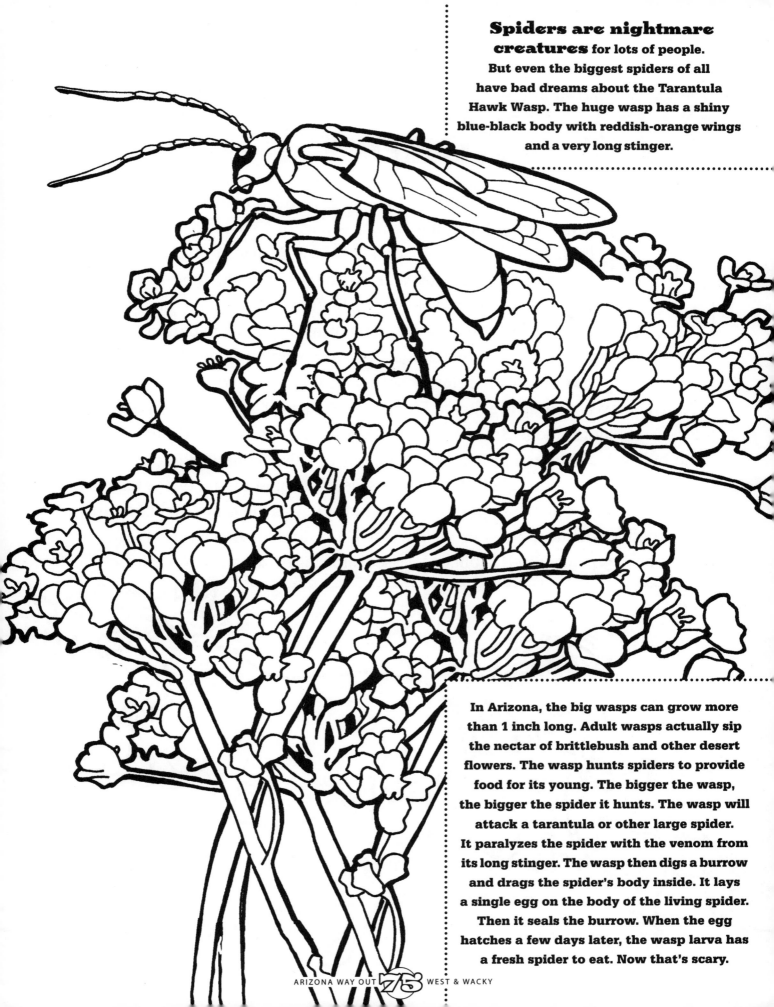

Spiders are nightmare creatures for lots of people. But even the biggest spiders of all have bad dreams about the Tarantula Hawk Wasp. The huge wasp has a shiny blue-black body with reddish-orange wings and a very long stinger.

In Arizona, the big wasps can grow more than 1 inch long. Adult wasps actually sip the nectar of brittlebush and other desert flowers. The wasp hunts spiders to provide food for its young. The bigger the wasp, the bigger the spider it hunts. The wasp will attack a tarantula or other large spider. It paralyzes the spider with the venom from its long stinger. The wasp then digs a burrow and drags the spider's body inside. It lays a single egg on the body of the living spider. Then it seals the burrow. When the egg hatches a few days later, the wasp larva has a fresh spider to eat. Now that's scary.

STATEHOOD! A LONG ROAD

IT TOOK 62 YEARS FOR ARIZONA to become a state. In 1850, it was admitted to the Union as part of New Mexico Territory. In 1863, it became Arizona Territory. Finally in 1912, Arizona became the 48th state. ☆ Arizonans thought their territory would become a state in 1898. They volunteered in droves to fight in the Spanish-American War. They did it in part to prove how serious they were about statehood. They also wanted to show how loyal they were to the Union. Their fervor soon had them labeled Rough Riders. ☆ The bravest among the Rough Riders was Buckey O'Neill. He was known for his ability to dodge Spanish bullets. Other officers fell around him. But, the bullets just whizzed past O'Neill. One day as O'Neill charged into battle, he said, "Who wouldn't gladly lay down his life to put another star on the flag?" Very shortly after that, a sniper's bullet hit him. He was the only officer in the Rough Riders to die in the war. ☆ Still, the Union told Arizona it wasn't ready to admit them. But in 1904, a bill was passed allowing Arizona and New Mexico

to merge into one big state. The new state would be called Arizona. The capital would be Santa Fe. Even though it would have made Arizona the third largest state in the country, they didn't agree. ✰ By 1911, Arizona was one law away from becoming a state. President William Howard Taft said he wouldn't accept Arizona's constitution unless we removed the recalling of judges. After plenty of grumbling and debating, Arizona finally agreed. ✰ Arizona was supposed to officially become a state on February 12, 1912. But that was Abraham Lincoln's birthday and a federal holiday. They couldn't do it on February 13 either. Taft said it would be bad luck. So the official date of statehood for Arizona was February 14, 1912. Arizona was the Valentine's State. ✰ Arizonans celebrated with fireworks, parades, and bell ringing. There was even supposed to be a 48-gun salute. But it had to stop after 38 shots because it was breaking windows and scaring horses. Now that's wacky!

Nobody celebrated Arizona statehood louder than the good folks of Bisbee. They set off a charge of dynamite that almost blew off the top of a mountain.

COLOR ME ARIZONA

ARIZONA'S
STATE
STUFF

Saguaro Cactus Blossom
ARIZONA'S STATE FLOWER

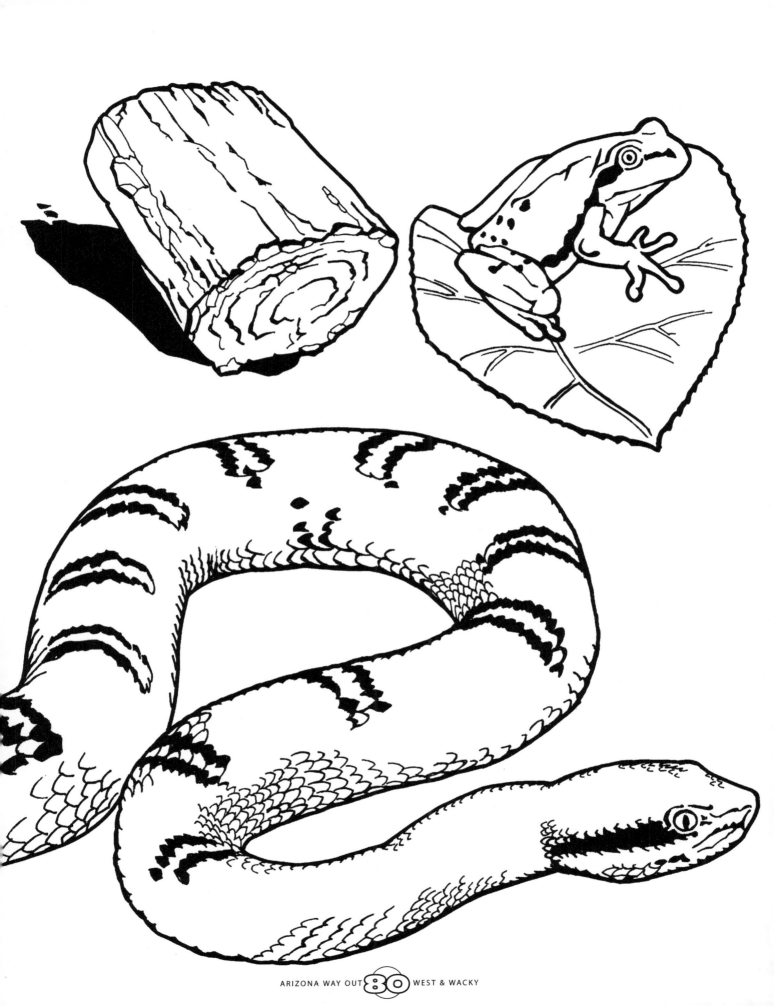

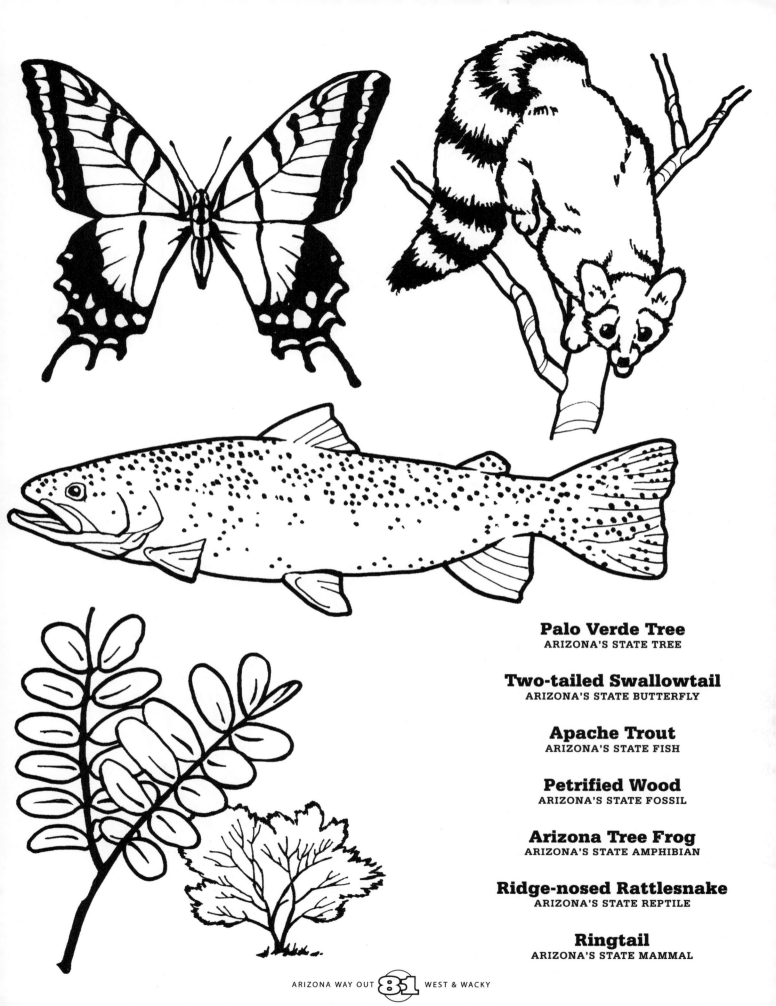

Palo Verde Tree
ARIZONA'S STATE TREE

Two-tailed Swallowtail
ARIZONA'S STATE BUTTERFLY

Apache Trout
ARIZONA'S STATE FISH

Petrified Wood
ARIZONA'S STATE FOSSIL

Arizona Tree Frog
ARIZONA'S STATE AMPHIBIAN

Ridge-nosed Rattlesnake
ARIZONA'S STATE REPTILE

Ringtail
ARIZONA'S STATE MAMMAL

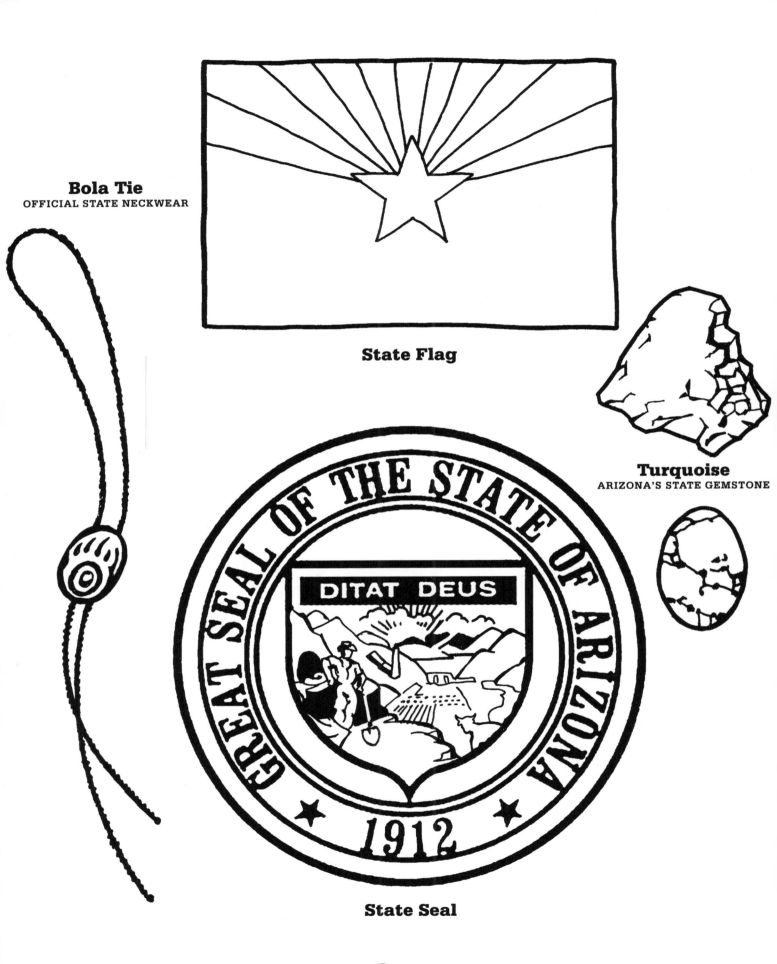

Bola Tie
OFFICIAL STATE NECKWEAR

State Flag

Turquoise
ARIZONA'S STATE GEMSTONE

GREAT SEAL OF THE STATE OF ARIZONA

DITAT DEUS

1912

State Seal

EYE ON THE CAPITAL

AS THE STORY GOES, if it wasn't for a glass eye, the capital of Arizona would be Prescott. But before we spill the beans on how Prescott lost being the state capital, we first need to tell you it WAS the capital. Are you confused yet? The first person appointed as Arizona Territory's governor was John Gurley. He was called a "lame duck," because he died before taking office. His replacement was John Goodwin. He and three judges set up a temporary capital at Camp Whipple. (Later, they named it Fort Whipple). In August of 1864, the men traveled south, taking the capital with them. They moved into the governor's mansion. It was a log structure on Gurley Street. Today, that building is Sharlot Hall Museum. They decided to call the town Prescott. Prescott enjoyed being the state capital for only three years. Powerful legislators were able to get the capital moved to Tucson, the "Old Pueblo." In 1877, 10 years after Tucson became the capital, Prescott got it back.

In 1889, Phoenix was growing so fast its residents were able to persuade lawmakers to move the capital to the Valley of the Sun. But, it was only decided by one vote…

As the story goes, a wacky incident happened the night before the legislative vote decided the locations of the state capital. It is said that a delegate favoring Prescott took his glass eye out and put it in a glass of water like he always did. But the next morning, he discovered his female companion had actually swallowed the eye. She unknowingly drank the water with the eyeball in it. The man was so vain he refused to attend the voting session. Because Prescott lost his vote, Phoenix captured the capital by one vote!

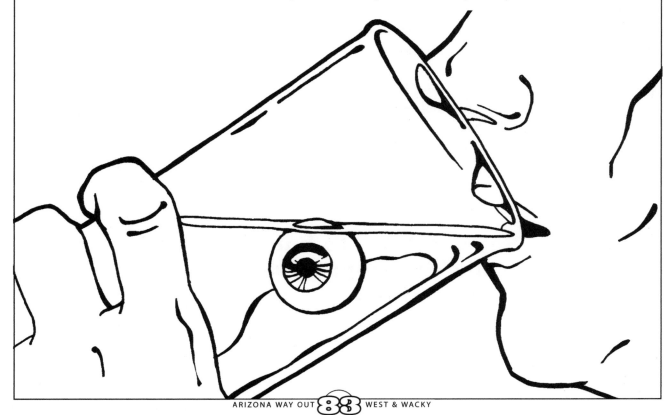

GROWING STUFF IN THE DESERT

ASK SOMEONE WHO HAS NEVER SEEN ARIZONA to tell you what they think it might look like. Chances are they would describe the land as dried out clay or miles of lifeless sand. But ask Arizona farmers to describe their land, and they might say, "lush, green fields." What a wacky way to describe the desert! ☆ Arizona is the fourth driest state in the country. On average, it rains less than 14 inches per year. How can Arizona have lush farmland? Agriculture in Arizona is a $10 billion industry. How can that be? ☆ Today we have dams to prevent rivers from running dry. We have human-made lakes to store water. And, like the Hohokam, we use canals to channel water where we want it to go. We also send water through pipes. This makes it possible to water crops and livestock. ☆ Arizona ranks second in the nation for producing cantaloupe and honeydew melons, broccoli, cauliflower, spinach, lemons, head and leaf lettuce. In fact, Yuma, Arizona is the "winter lettuce capital of the world."

Arizona's first farmers were the Anasazi. They lived in northwest Arizona 2,000 years ago. They grew corn, beans, and squash. In A.D. 300, the Hohokam moved to central Arizona from Mexico. They grew squash, beans, and cotton. The Hohokam used ditches to direct water from rivers to their crops. Today, we call it irrigation.
Sadly, a long drought made it hard for them to grow food. Many of the Anasazi and Hohokam died. So, in A.D. 1300, they moved out of the area in search of water.

Hey Kids! Try to find these hidden objects in this drawing: olive, apple, pair of jeans, latex glove, lemon, broccoli, egg, cantaloupe, hamburger

Arizona's farmers grow enough cotton every year to make more than one pair of jeans for every American. They grow enough grapefruit to give each person in the United States half of a grapefruit a day. Each year, the chickens in Arizona lay about 60 eggs for every resident. And, ranchers produce enough beef for every person living in Arizona to have a ¼-pound burger 300 days a year! Hay, oranges, apples, dates, olives, and pecans also grow in Arizona. Scientists at the Maricopa Agricultural Center are studying how to better grow guayule (sounds like wah-YOO-lay). The plant is known for making latex that is hypoallergenic. That means people aren't allergic to it. Latex is used to make the gloves doctors and dentists wear.

How to Make Nutty Ink

In the area around Green Valley, Arizona, 8 million pounds of pecans are picked from about 106,000 trees. In addition to eating the yummy nuts, early American colonists used pecans to make ink. Here's how you can make your own nutty ink!

INGREDIENTS: 8 whole pecan shells
1 cup water
½ teaspoon vinegar
½ teaspoon of salt

Place the shells in a thick zip-top plastic bag or wrap them in cloth.
Pound them with a hammer until they are broken into very small pieces.

Put one cup of water in a saucepan, and add the crushed shells. Bring the water to a boil.
Turn down the heat to a low temperature, and simmer for 30 to 45 minutes.
The water should be a dark brown.

Remove the pan from the stove and allow
the liquid to cool. Put a fine strainer over
a glass jar and pour the liquid into the jar.

Add ½ teaspoon of vinegar, which keeps the ink from fading.
Add ½ teaspoon of salt to the ink. This keeps it from molding.

Screw the lid tightly on the jar, and shake it up to dissolve salt.

Your nutty ink is ready to use with a feather quill, paint brush,
or old-fashioned ink pen nib.

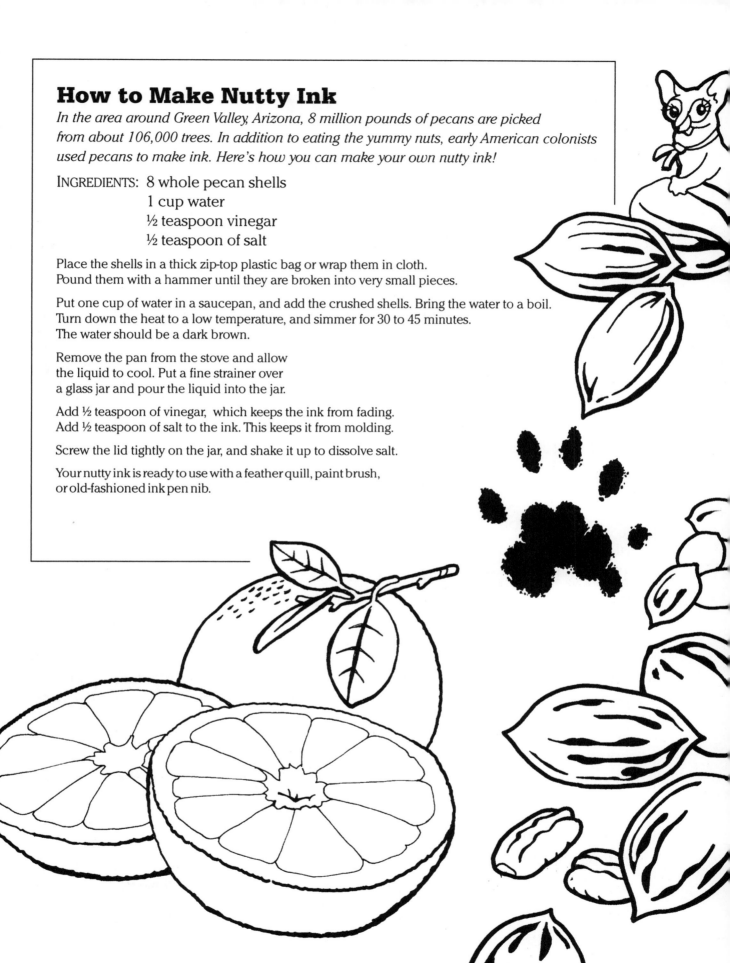

SHAKE, RATTLE & ROLL

THE NEW VALLEY METRO LIGHT RAIL started running trains in December 2008. The system serves riders in the cities of Phoenix, Tempe, and Mesa. During its first two days of operation, more than 200,000 people road the sleek silver electric trains. ☆ But guess what? Streetcars that use electric power to move on tracks are not new to Arizona. Phoenix had a light rail system in 1893. Tucson got one in 1906. Riders liked the electric rail cars. They could rely on them, and they made better time than animals. Plus, streetcars didn't poop on the road! It was not long before street railway cars replaced all mule and horse-drawn cars in Arizona's biggest towns. So why did electric rail cars all but disappear in Arizona? And, why did they come back? ☆ The first automobile arrived in Tucson in 1900. Cars let people come and go as they wished. Driving was fun, too! Soon, crude roads popped up from city to city. In 1916, wood planks were used to build a highway near Yuma. The one-lane plank road helped drivers cross the sandy desert into California. But the hot desert sun, wind, and sand warped the wood. That made the roadway bumpy. Cars could only drive 10 miles per hour. Drivers nicknamed the road "Old Shaky." ☆ In 1925, the United States started building highways across the country. By 1926, drivers could use Interstate 8 instead of the nasty plank road. By 1938, drivers could travel on Route 66. Paved roads took them from Chicago all the way to Los Angeles. Route 66 cut straight through Arizona. Holbrook, Winslow, Flagstaff, and Williams are all part of the famed route. ☆ In the late 1920s, people began to ride the bus. Busses also led to the demise of the street railcars. They were quieter, and they didn't need tracks. Cities could create bus systems

---

MORE MOVING FACTS

1852 Steamboats are used on the Colorado River.

1857 First stagecoach in Arizona.

1887 The first passenger train arrives in Tempe on June 19.

1887 The first passenger train comes to Phoenix.

1895 The first passenger train links Ash Fork, Prescott, Wickenburg, Glendale, and Phoenix.

1919 The first government-owned airport in the United States is dedicated in Tucson.

that served more riders for less money. By 1940, a decision was made to replace streetcars and start a Valleywide bus system. The last of the streetcars ended operations in 1948. ☆ For many years, Arizona enjoyed cars and busses with gasoline engines. Arizona's population grew to almost 6 million people. More people meant more drivers. More drivers meant more pollution from vehicles that run on gasoline. To cut back on pollution, some of Arizona's city leaders thought about going back to electric rail cars. ☆ By 2002, Tempe unveiled its plan for a light rail system. Soon, Phoenix, Glendale, Mesa, and Chandler all began plans for light rail. As the price of gasoline continues to rise, more and more people are riding the new trains each year. An idea that worked well more than a century ago is working again. Now that's a good kind of wacky!

Ghosts of Canyon Diablo: People say that Canyon Diablo is haunted. It is haunted by a rugged and violent history. The name means Devil's Canyon. During the early 1880s, the Santa Fe Railroad needed to build a bridge to cross the canyon. At first, survey teams said it could not be done. It took several attempts, but a spectacular bridge was finally built. The town of Canyon Diablo grew up around the railroad camp. It was a wild place. Gunfights were common. Some say the place was rougher than Tombstone. Today it is a ghost town. But trains still use the bridge to cross Canyon Diablo.

WHAT PART OF THE CAR IS THE LAZIEST?

T _ _   _ _ _ _ _ _   _ _ C A _ _ _   T _ _ _
4 19 17   6 19 17 17 13 24   21 17 20 14 2 24 17   4 19 17 22

A _ _   A _ _ A _ _   T _ _ _ _
14 9 17   14 13 6 14 22 24   4 8 9 17 11

A	B	C	D	E	F	G	H	I	J	K	L	M	N	O	P	Q	R	S	T	U	V	W	X	Y	Z
14		20																	4						

To find the answer, you have to break the secret code! Each letter of the alphabet is equal to only one number. For example, T=4, so wherever there is a space with a 4 below, we put a T in the space. C=20, so we put a C wherever there is a 20, and A=14, so wherever there is a 14, we put an A.

Now break the rest of the secret code by answering the questions. Put the answers in the boxes provided. When you fill in a letter over a number in an answer, put that number under the letter boxes in the line above. You make the key to let you solve the riddle. *Hint: All the answers are found in "Shake, Rattle, and Roll."*

What was the nickname
of the wood plank road used in 1916? ⬜⬜⬜ ⬜⬜⬜⬜⬜
                                                  19   22

The hot desert sun made the wood plank road ⬜⬜⬜⬜⬜ .
                                                              21

The first automobile in Arizona was delivered to ⬜⬜⬜⬜⬜⬜ .
                                                                     24

In Arizona, Route 66 goes
through Holbrook, Winslow, Flagstaff, and ⬜⬜⬜⬜⬜⬜⬜ .
                                              6   8

Although Arizona's last electric streetcars stopped running in 1948, city leaders brought back electric rail cars to cut down on ⬜⬜⬜⬜⬜⬜⬜⬜⬜ .
                                         13   2

As Arizona's population grows, more people traveling creates more ⬜⬜⬜⬜⬜⬜⬜ ,
which means more pollution from vehicles that run on gasoline.
                                       11   17

Both streetcars and
the Valley Metro Light Rail are powered by ⬜⬜⬜⬜⬜⬜⬜⬜⬜⬜⬜ .
                                                       9

HOW MANY?

OVER A 100-YEAR SPAN, the number of people in Arizona shot up 4,000 percent! That happened between the years 1900 and 2000. Such wacky growth made Arizona the second fastest growing state in America. Nevada took first place. It grew 12 percent more than Arizona. ☆ As of 2010, 24 percent more people lived in Arizona than in 2000. That put Arizona's growth in second place for the decade. Once again, Nevada was the fastest growing state. It had 35 percent more people in those 10 years. ☆ Being one of the fastest growing states does not mean Arizona had the most people. ☆ In 2010, Arizona had a little more than 6 million people. That ranked Arizona as the 16th most populated state in the country. California took first place. It had a little more than 37 million people. ☆

More interesting facts from the Census Bureau:

In 1900, about 40,000 people younger than age 15 lived in Arizona.
In 2000, the state had more than a million people younger than 15.

In 1900, Arizona had about 51,000 females. In 2000, that total grew to more than 2 million gals.

In 1900, Arizona had almost 72,000 males. In 2000, there were more than 2 million guys.

In 2000, more than 1 million Arizonans lived in houses they owned.
In 1900, there were only about 15,000 people living in houses they owned.

You might wonder where on Earth all these numbers come from. They come from the U.S. Census Bureau. Their job is to count and survey all the people living in the country. Every 10 years, Census results tell us all kinds of details about our population. We learn the race of the people who were counted. Whether they own a house or rent one. We also learn the ages of all the people living in the country. We learn whether residents are boys or girls, and a whole lot more.

COUNTING ON ARIZONA

All the words listed to the right of the grid have something to do with Arizona
and its population. See if you can find the words in the letter grid.
They can run across, up and down, diagonally, forwards, or backwards.

```
I  G  J  E  L  C  O  W  B  S  N  S  P  M  S
A  K  L  N  I  V  R  D  V  E  U  O  W  Z  B
T  N  E  D  I  S  E  R  Z  S  P  R  B  B  C
K  G  O  H  G  T  E  I  N  U  C  S  V  I  C
E  N  B  Z  A  V  T  E  L  L  S  S  O  E  H
C  E  A  I  I  I  C  A  T  E  S  U  O  H  Y
A  S  L  R  C  R  T  X  N  P  O  T  N  C  W
R  S  V  T  Y  I  A  M  E  R  I  C  A  O  W
D  M  N  B  O  J  O  K  C  C  R  O  Z  U  P
Z  E  I  N  V  H  N  S  R  O  E  L  F  N  C
R  A  W  L  J  X  T  I  E  U  B  E  X  T  B
X  X  Y  N  L  A  V  W  P  N  M  J  Z  G  H
X  S  K  D  T  I  X  J  O  T  U  A  G  E  N
O  N  E  E  L  P  O  E  P  R  N  K  H  I  Y
X  D  E  C  A  D  E  N  Y  Y  G  J  B  Z  N
```

AGE
ARIZONA
CITIZEN
COUNTRY
DETAILS
HOUSE
NUMBER
PERCENT
RACE
RENT
STATE
AMERICA
CENSUS
COUNT
DECADE
GROWTH
MILLION
PEOPLE
POPULATION
RANK
RESIDENT
SURVEY

LISTEN CLOSE! Do you hear that loud cackling call? *ka-KAA-ka-ka*. It repeats. *Ka-KAA-ka-ka*. Yep, that is a Gambel's Quail. Probably a male bird calling from high inside the safety of a desert bush. The quail's call is an unmistakable sound of the Southwest deserts. The short-legged, pear-shaped birds are easy to recognize. They have a black, tear-shaped plume on top of a chestnut brown head. The male has a gleaming black face framed in white with rusty sides and diagonal stripes. Watch for them in the early spring when the desert is cool and water is flowing. Groups of quail are called coveys. The babies skitter along in a long line behind their plump mother. They look like a string of beads as they run for cover in the thorny brush.

Tiger Beetles look like brightly colored jewels flashing across the desert floor. All Tiger Beetles are hunters. They have excellent eyesight, long legs, and are very fast runners. In Arizona, some Tiger Beetles hunt for only a few hours each day. When the temperature gets too hot, they look for a shady spot to cool down.

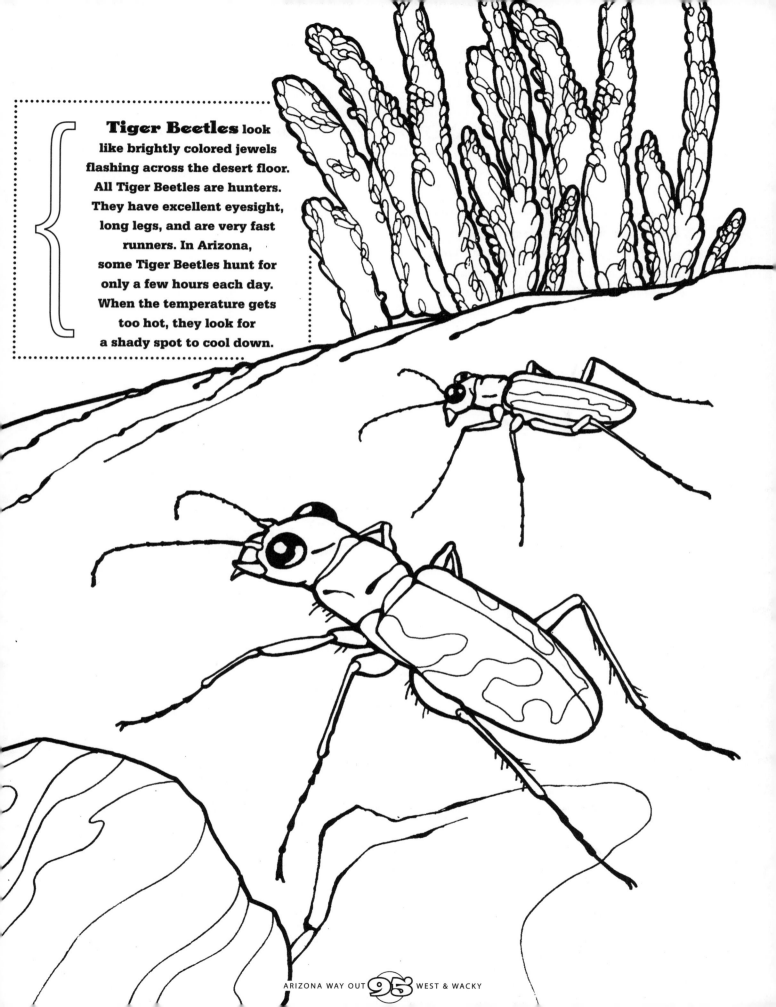

The funnel-shaped flowers of an Organ Pipe Cactus only open at night. The plant's round, red, spiny fruit is considered the best tasting of all cactus fruits. The Pima and Tohono O'odham people would travel hundreds of miles to harvest Organ Pipe fruits.

The lone Coyote howling at the moon is a symbol of the American West. But coyotes are not solitary animals. The critters love to talk. Coyotes use at least 10 different sounds to communicate, including barks, yips, growls, and howls. No texting for them.

So much for the honeymoon... "Hey boy, I'd really like to meet ya. But, hmmmm, you're looking so gooooood...I might just have to eat ya!" said the Black Widow Spider to her newest mate. It's true, the black widow is one of the most feared of all spiders. It has powerful venom that is extremely painful for humans. And the female spiders do eat their mates...but not always. They'd much rather dine on insects trapped in their sticky, tangled webs.

VISITING THE WILD, WACKY WEST

MORE THAN 35 MILLION local and international visitors come to Arizona each year. Combined, they spend more than $16 billion per year. All that visiting and spending creates more than 157,000 jobs. What kind of strange, wacky or wonderful things might bring travelers to the state? ☆ The Grand Canyon is an obvious answer. In 1919, when the Grand Canyon first became a national park, there were 44,173 visitors. Today, more than 5 million take a trip to the canyon in a given year. ☆ So what brings people from all over the world to this big hole in the ground? The sheer size of the hole for one thing! The Grand Canyon is 277 miles long. A football field is only 100 yards long. That would make the Grand Canyon about 4,875 football fields long! At its widest point, the canyon is 18 miles wide. (You figure out how many football fields that is!) ☆ The deepest point of the Grand Canyon is 6,000 feet. The average female teacher is 5 feet, 4 inches tall. That means it would take about 1,125 teachers standing on each other's heads to go from the bottom to the top! ☆ One would think the Grand Canyon was named "Grand" because of its grandiose size. Others think it was named for its grand beauty. But, the Colorado River runs

The rangers who work at Grand Canyon National Park have a good tip for the millions of people who visit each year. If you plan to hike into or around the Grand Canyon, remember— it's NOT Disneyland! Plan ahead. Hike smart. The rangers say the difference between a great hike and a trip to the hospital is really up to you.

at the bottom of the Grand Canyon. And, a long time ago, it was called the Grand River. Some researchers say the "Grand" comes from the river's name. It took 17 million years for the river's waters to erode the canyon into what you see today—no matter what you call it. ☆ For as long as anyone can remember, people have come to the Grand Canyon to hike, raft the river, and just admire its awesome beauty. However, one thing visitors couldn't do in 1919 that they can do today is the Skywalk. This horseshoe shaped, steel framed overlook has a glass floor and sides. The lookout jets out about 70 feet from the canyon rim. Talk about a view!

Riding the Rapids

Every year, thousands of people ride rafts and kayaks down the Colorado River through the Grand Canyon. This stretch of river boasts some of the wildest whitewater and biggest rapids in North America.

Have I been here before?

Monument Valley is a stunning, beautiful place. If you visit, you'll probably feel as if you've been there before. You have. Not physically. But anyone who has ever seen an old Western movie knows the shapes of the craggy red sandstone buttes that tower into a clear blue sky. Hollywood has used Monument Valley as the dramatic landscape in lots of movies. It was John Ford's favorite place on Earth to make films. In 1939, the famous director filmed Stagecoach in Monument Valley. The movie made a star out of a young actor named John Wayne.

Red rocks!

Visitors from all over the world come to see Sedona's ancient ruins and awesome red rock formations. There's one in the shape of a coffee pot. One looks like a tea pot. Another looks like a large bell. There are even some that look like giant cow patties!

☆ Most people agree a visit to Sedona makes them feel refreshed. Some say it's the natural beauty that pleases them. Others say the hiking and jeep tours make them feel good. Still, others insist it's the mystical energy from the red sandstone that lifts their mood. They call those energy pockets vortexes. Not everyone agrees that vortexes actually exist. But they all agree Sedona is worth the trip!

Girl power

Sharlot Hall was the first woman in Arizona to hold a political office. In 1909, she was appointed territorial historian. That was in 1914, before women were allowed to vote in Arizona. She was also a writer and a poet. ☆ In 1924, Hall was asked to represent the state in the Electoral College. But she didn't have enough money to buy the proper clothes. So, she declined the offer. However, officials at the United Verde Mine in Jerome decided to help her. They pitched in to buy her a blue silk dress and copper mesh coat.

Her clothes were a hit back East! ☆ When Hall went back home, she asked for help to restore the first governor's mansion. It was built in 1864. It took Hall until 1928 to get the job done. Today, the building is called the Sharlot Hall Museum. People come from all over to see it. In addition to the mansion, they can see Victorian treasures. Guests can also view Native American baskets, a vintage stagecoach, and many old photos and papers. ☆ In 1981, Hall was among the first to be inducted into the Arizona Women's Hall of Fame.

Step aside Spiderman!

Spider Woman existed long before the comic book character Spiderman. There is a huge rock spire in Canyon de Chelly called Spider Rock. It jets up 800 feet tall and is one of many sites in the canyon Navajo people consider sacred. The Navajo deity Spider Woman is said to live on the top of the rock. They say she gives power to those who destroy evil. But, she also punishes those who cause evil. As legend goes, she punishes naughty children, too. She crawls down from her nesting place to grab offenders. She brings them up to the top and leaves them there. If you look at the top of Spider Rock, you will see white, chalky rocks. Those are said to be the children's bones.

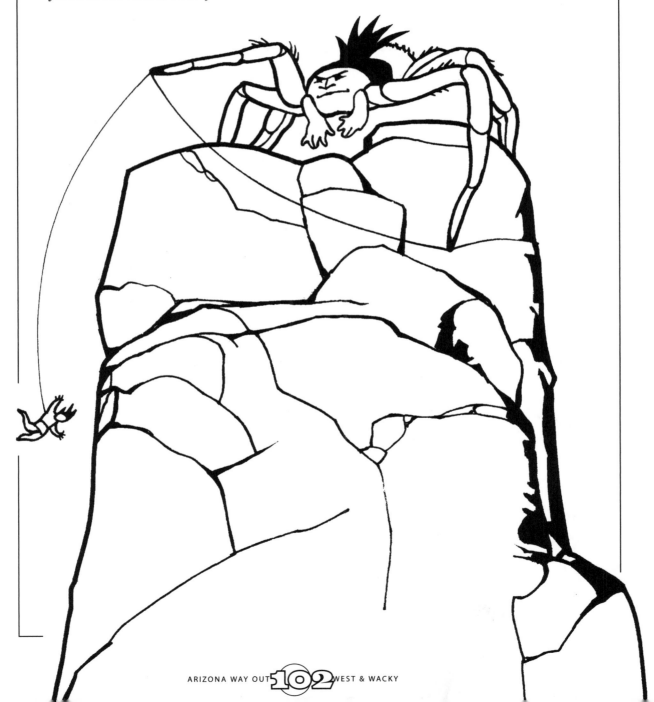

Knowing the name of a place is important. Arizona's native peoples have names for special places. But it can be tough to translate those names into other languages. Canyon de Chelly National Monument is such a place. The Navajo people call the area Tsaile or Tsegi, pronounced as *SAY-ih*. The word means "canyon" or "inside the rock." Spanish explorers heard the Navajo word as "Chelly." They pronounced it as CHAY-yi. Then, for some reason, the pronunciation changed to de-SHAY, a much more French version. No matter how you say it, Canyon de Chelly is a spectacular place to visit.

Old Tucson, or is it?

Tourists flock to Old Tucson Studios. More than 300 films and television projects were filmed there. Unlike the name indicates, however, Old Tucson Studios was not the site of old Tucson. It was built in 1939 to film the movie "Arizona." ☆ Since then, an A-list of movie stars has filmed there. They include: Paul Newman, John Wayne, Glenn Ford, Burt Lancaster, Kurt Russell, Val Kilmer, Cuba Gooding Jr., Sharon Stone, Clint Eastwood and many, many more. ☆ Another wacky fact about Old Tucson Studios is that "Gunfight at O.K. Corral" was filmed there–not in Tombstone. Both the 1993 movie "Tombstone" and the 1957 "Gunfight at O.K. Corral" were shot on site instead of in Tombstone. Plus, the famous gunfight between Doc Holliday and the three Earp brothers against Billy Claiborne, the Clanton brothers, and the two McLaury boys happened on a vacant lot. That lot was a block away from the real O.K. Corral on Fremont Street in Tombstone. It lasted 24 seconds and 30 shots were fired. But, "Gunfight on the Empty Lot" doesn't sound very good. So, Hollywood changed it to "Gunfight at O.K. Corral." ☆ So, if you go to Tombstone, you won't see the movie set location for the gunfight at O.K. Corral. And, if you go to the O.K. Corral, you won't see the location of the real gunfight either. That's so wacky it hurts your brain just to think about it!

Keeping history alive

Tombstone is a "living" piece of history. Historic buildings, people dressed in period costumes, and staged gunfights make visitors feel like they stepped back in time. ☆ Arizona's most famous cemetery is in Tombstone. It's called Boothill Graveyard. Many gunfight victims are buried there including Billy Clanton and Tom and Frank McLaury from the infamous 1881 Fremont Street shootout. Billy Claiborne is buried at Boothill, too. But he died in a gunfight in Tombstone in 1882. ☆ For more "live" history, visit the Pioneer Living History Village in Phoenix. The re-created 1800s town is on 90 acres of land. Actors roam the streets portraying town folk and gunfighters. All the structures are real historical buildings that have been moved there and restored. ☆ See an 1890s dress shop. Venture inside a pioneer church and schoolhouse. Visit a blacksmith shop. Peek in the Sheriff's office, and see the three grand chandeliers in the opera house. By the time this book comes out, there should even be an old-time bakery to visit. ☆ In central Phoenix, history lovers can visit historic Heritage Square. The cornerstone of the square is the Rosson House Museum. The Rosson House was built in 1895. It was bought by the City of Phoenix in 1974. Since then, it has been restored and now offers tours. The Rosson House Museum is in the Carriage House. ☆ Heritage Square's Hands-On Heritage House offers fun activities and exhibits for kids and adults. It was originally built in 1901 as a rental property. Also built in 1901 was the New York Store. Today it is home to the Arizona Doll & Toy Museum. Visitors can see toys from the past and imagine children playing with them. Turn to Page 56 to learn about a few of the wacky playthings kids used to call fun!

Note: For information on interests in Wickenburg and Yuma, see "The Legal Frontier," beginning on Page 70.

Busy skies: Phoenix is a large city. In 2011, it ranked as the sixth biggest city in the United States. Phoenix also is home to one of the country's busiest airports. In 2010, more than 1 million planes took off and landed at Sky Harbor Airport. More than 40 million passengers landed in Phoenix. Some were coming home. Some to visit. Others were on their way to other places. It wasn't always that way. Sky Harbor Airport was built in 1928. But it was so isolated from the city that people called it "The Farm." You won't find any vegetables growing there today. Just lots and lots of people and planes.

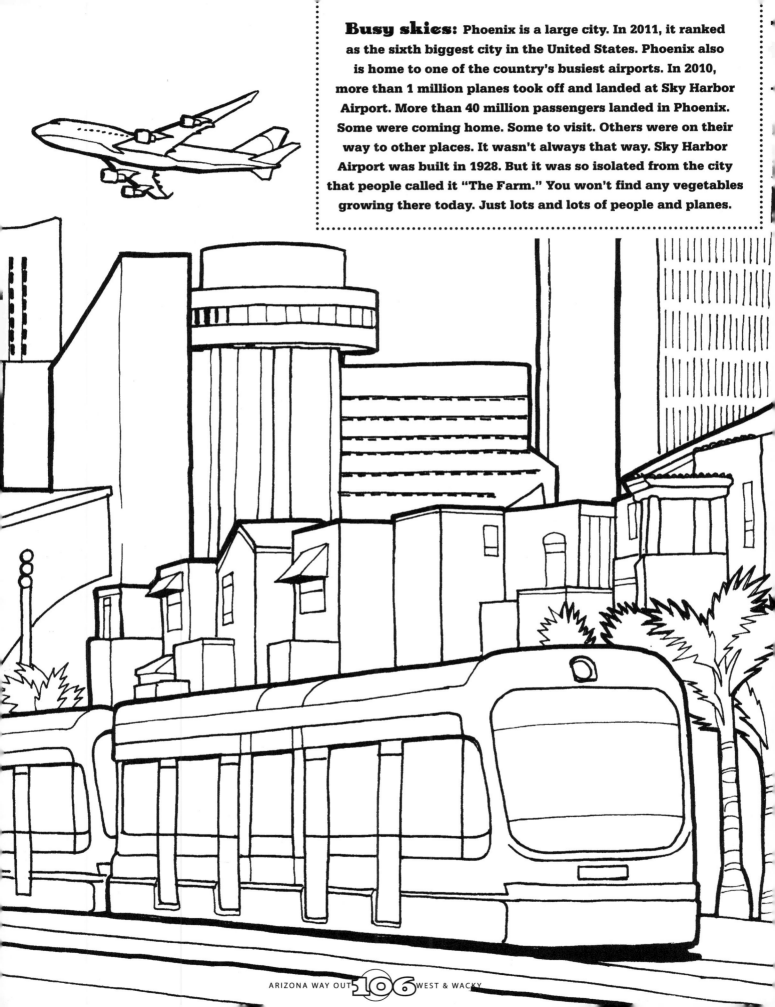

Touring Arizona

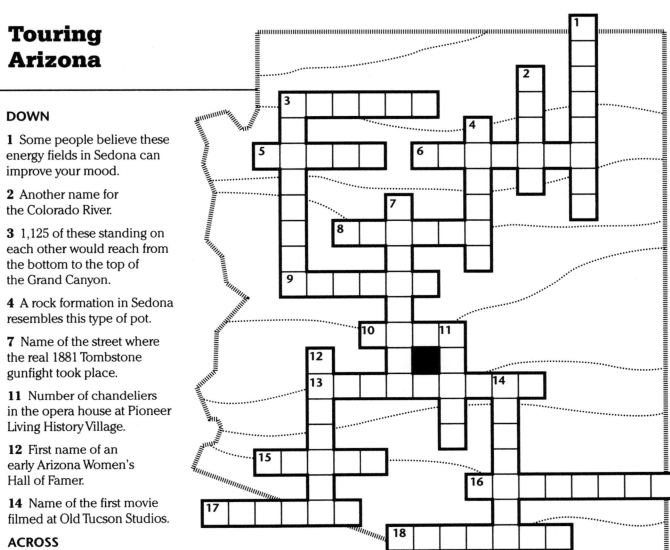

DOWN

1 Some people believe these energy fields in Sedona can improve your mood.

2 Another name for the Colorado River.

3 1,125 of these standing on each other would reach from the bottom to the top of the Grand Canyon.

4 A rock formation in Sedona resembles this type of pot.

7 Name of the street where the real 1881 Tombstone gunfight took place.

11 Number of chandeliers in the opera house at Pioneer Living History Village.

12 First name of an early Arizona Women's Hall of Famer.

14 Name of the first movie filmed at Old Tucson Studios.

ACROSS

3 Name of the city where both the 1993 and 1956 movies about the shootout at the O.K. Corral were filmed.

5 It eroded the Grand Canyon into the big gorge you see today.

6 The city that purchased the Rosson House and restored it.

8 The city in which the United Verde Mine is located.

9 According to Navajo lore, this creature punishes those who cause evil.

10 Sharlot Hall was a writer, historian, and what else?

13 The first territorial political office held by an Arizona woman.

15 The first name of the Claiborne brother who did *not* die in the famous 1881 Tombstone gunfight.

16 Cemetery in Tombstone where famous gunfighters are buried.

17 Number of shots fired during the Freemont Street gunfight.

18 Horseshoe shaped thing you can walk on today that you couldn't walk on in 1919 when the Grand Canyon became a National Park.

GLOSSARY

Note: This glossary defines words found in *Arizona Way Out West & Wacky*. Sometimes words have more than one meaning. Even so, this glossary only tells what a word means as it relates to this book. Use the dictionary to find more definitions.

AC See air conditioning.

air conditioning also air conditioner. A device for cooling the air and controlling its humidity.

adobe (uh-DOH-bee) A mixture of clay and straw used for making bricks or blocks that are dried in the sun. Adobe bricks are used for buildings and fencing.

agave (uh-GAH-vee) A plant with stiff, fleshy, sword-shaped leaves with spiny edges known for growing in the American Southwest.

aggressive (uh-GRES-iv) Showing a readiness to attack others.

agriculture (AG-ri-kuhl-chur) The producing of crops and raising of livestock.

antennae (an-TEN-ay) Threadlike movable feelers on the heads of insects. One antennae is called an antenna.

arid (AIR-id) Extremely dry.

Arizona Revised Statutes The list of documented laws in the State of Arizona.

bacteria (bak-TEER-ee-uh) Bacteria grows in food that is spoiled. Bacteria are microscopic, single-cell living things that can cause disease in humans.

burrow (BUHR-oh) A hole in the ground made by an animal.

canal (kuh-NAL) A waterway built by people used to direct water for irrigation or to water crops.

Canyon·de Chelly (KAN-yun deh SHAY) A reservation in northeast Arizona containing cliff-dweller ruins and beautiful red rock formations.

census (SEN-suhs) An official count of all the people living in a country or area.

Census Bureau The agency in charge of counting the number of people in a country, city or town.

chandelier (shan-duh-LEER) A lighting fixture that hangs from a ceiling. It usually has many small lights on several branches.

City Council A group of people who pass laws regulating cities or towns. They manage the city or town's funds.

committee (kuh-MIT-ee) A group of persons chosen or elected to perform a duty, study a subject or consider a subject.

community (kuh-MYOO-ni-tee) The place and the people who live in it.

constitution (kahn-sti-TOO-shuhn) The laws of a state or nation that establish the powers and duties of the government and guarantee certain rights to people in that state or nation.

cornerstone (KOR-nur stohn) The main support or focal point of a building. The most essential or important part of something.

cornhusk (KORN-huhsk) The husk or greenery directly attached to the outside of an ear of corn that turns brownish-yellow when dried. The husks are not the leaves on a cornstalk.

crude (KROOD) Rough, not very refined. Primitive.

decade (DEK-ayd) A period of 10 years.

demise (deh-MIHZ) End of. Death of.

dwellers (DWEL-uhrs) People or beings that live in an area for a while.

Electoral College A body of people chosen by voters in each state to elect the president and vice-president of the United States.

geologist (jee-ah-LAH-jist) A scientist who studies the physical structure of the Earth, especially its layers of soil and rock.

hexagonal (hek-SAG-uh-nuhl) Having the shape of a hexagon, which has six angles and six sides.

Hohokam (HOH-hoh-kahm) A prehistoric desert culture of the American Southwest centering in the Gila Valley area of Arizona. The Hohokam people were known for using irrigation to grow crops. They built Arizona's original canals.

hostage (hah-stij) A person who is kept prisoner by a person who demands something before the captured person is released.

javelina (hah-vuh-LEE-nuh) A collared peccary. The animal has thick, bristly black and gray hair covering its muscular body. A band of grayish-white fur runs from shoulder to shoulder. Although it looks like a wild boar, it is not.

lard (LAHRD) The soft, white fat from the fatty tissue of the hog.

legend (LEJ-uhnd) An old story that is widely believed even though it can't be proven as true.

lethal (LEE-thuhl) Deadly, fatal.

memoir (MEM-wahr) A true story one writes about oneself.

mesquite (meh-SKEET) A shrub or small tree found in the American Southwest and Mexico.

mill (MIL) A building in which grain is ground into flour.

molt (MOHLT) To shed old skin, fur, hair or feathers so that new ones can grow.

mythical (MITH-i-kuhl) Based on a myth or story that is not proven. Myths are like legends, usually believed by many. Imaginary.

Navajo (NAV-uh-hoh) A member of the largest group of Native American people living in the American Southwest. The Navajo reservation covers parts of Arizona, New Mexico, and Utah.

nocturnal (nahk-TUR-nuhl) Active at night rather than the daytime.

notorious (noh-TOR-ee-uhs) Widely known for some bad characteristic or bad action.

ocotillo (ohk-uh-TEE-oh) A spiny desert shrub that can grow quite tall. It has tight clusters of orange-red flowers at the tips of its branches and tiny green leaves.

penmanship Style or quality of handwriting. Writing with a pen.

pen name A false name that an author uses on his or her writings or work.

percent (pur-SENT) A part or fraction that is one one-hundredth; 10 percent is 10 out of 100 or 10 out of every 100 units. Percent is written using the symbol %.

pincer (PIN-sur) The pinching claw of an insect or arachnid.

poker (POH-kur) A card game in which each player bets on the value of his or her hand–or set of cards. Poker is a game of chance. Bets can be for money or for things such as land, a horse, etc.

pollution (puh-LOO-shuhn) Harmful materials that damage or contaminate the air, water, or soil.

population (pahp-yuh-LAY-shuhn) The total number of people living in an area such as a city or country. The people or things living in a certain place.

predator (PRED-uh-tur) An animal that lives by hunting and eating other animals for food. The animals it kills and eats are its prey.

prospector (PRAHS-pekt-uhr) A person who explores an area in search of valuable minerals such as gold, silver, copper, oil, etc.

provoke (pruh-VOHK) To annoy someone and make the person angry.

rehabilitate (ree-huh-BIL-uh-tayt) To restore to a former state. To restore to normal health or activity.

reservation (rez-ur-VAY-shuhn)
Land set apart for a special use as
for Native American people.

resident (REZ-i-duhnt) A person or being
that lives in a place for some length of time.

Ringtail Also known as Ringtail Cat or
Miner's Cat. Looking much like a skinny
raccoon, the Ringtail is Arizona's Official
Mammal. Ringtails are shy, nocturnal creatures
that miners treated as pets.

saguaro (suh-WARH-oh) A very tall cactus
with arms that grows in Arizona and neighboring
regions. It has an interior of long, woody ribs,
and an edible fruit.

scorpion (SKOR-pee-uhn) An arachnid
related to spiders. Scorpions have a long,
jointed body that ends in a long tail tipped
with a venomous stinger.

settlement (SET-uhl-muhnt) A small
village. A place or region where people stay
in one area.

smoke (SMOHK) **or smoked** To slowly
cook meat or other foods over burning wood
and/or coals in order to preserve it or give it
more flavor.

surrender (suh-REN-dur) To give oneself
up or give control to someone else.

streetcar A vehicle that carries people
from place to place and runs on rails, usually
on city streets and usually powered by electricity.

tarantula (tuh-RAN-chuh-luh) A large,
hairy spider found mainly in warm regions.
It does have fangs with venom, but is not
aggressive unless provoked.

unveil (uhn-VAYL) Uncover. To show or
make known to the public for the first time.

venomous (VEN-uhm-us)
Having or producing venom, which is poison.

yucca (YUHK-ah) A plant that grows in dry
regions like the American Southwest. It has
sharp, lance-shaped leaves and clusters of
white flowers that grow in vertical spikes.

Zuni (ZOO-nee) A group of Native Americans
that live in western New Mexico on Arizona's
eastern border.

Puzzle Answers and Keys

11 Silly Weather Jokes:
THE BIRDS HAVE
TO USE
POTHOLDERS TO
PULL WORMS OUT
OF THE GROUND

FARMERS ARE FEEDING
THEIR CHICKENS
CRUSHED ICE TO KEEP
THEM FROM LAYING
HARD-BOILED EGGS!

31 Geronimo: ONE WHO YAWNS

33 Cochise: HAVING THE STRENGTH OF OAK

55 Keeping Cool in the Desert:
NACHO CHEESE; ICE, AIR CONDITIONER, WATER,
POOL, POPSICLE, SHADE, MISTER, FAN, WET SHEETS,
SWAMP COOLER

65 Arizona Name Game:
1–TOMBSTONE, 2–PAGE, 3–MIAMI 4–SUPERIOR,
5–CAREFREE, 6–GLOBE, 7–KINGMAN,
8–SNOWFLAKE, 9–SURPRISE, 10–DEWEY

69 Gold, Greed and Mining Towns:
Across: 1–HANGING, 3–DOMINION, 5–HENRY,
6–FORTY, 8–CAVE IN, 10–TOMMYKNOCKERS,
11– VULTURE
Down: 2–ASSAY OFFICE, 4–ORE, 7–TIMBERS,
8–COPPER

91 What Part of the Car is Laziest?
THE WHEELS BECAUSE THEY ARE ALWAYS TIRED;
OLD SHAKY, BUMPY, TUCSON, WILLIAMS,
POLLUTION, DRIVERS, ELECTRICITY

107 Touring Arizona
Down: 1–VORTEXES, 2–GRAND, 3–TEACHERS,
4– COFFEE, 7–FREMONT, 11–THREE, 12–SHARLOT,
14–ARIZONA
Across: 3–TUCSON, 5–WATER, 6–PHOENIX, 8–JEROME,
9–SPIDER, 10–POET, 13–HISTORIAN, 15–BILLY,
16–BOOT HILL, 17–THIRTY, 18–SKYWALK

Solutions to picture puzzles:

9   Different Peaks

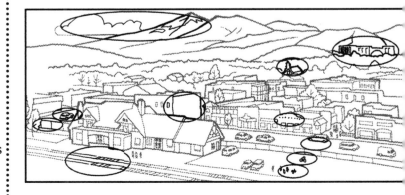

Conrad J. Storad is an award-winning author and Arizona's most popular writer of science and nature books for young readers. He has more than 40 titles to his credit. He also worked almost 25 years as director of Arizona State University's Office of Research Publications.

Lynda Exley is also a multi award-winning writer and editor. She has more than 15 years of experience working for well-known parenting magazines and newspapers such as *Arizona Parenting*, *Houston Parent*, *LA Parent* and *SanTan Sun News*. She is co-founder of KidsCanPublish.com.

Michael Hagelberg, award-winning illustrator and designer, was the creative director, designer and illustrator of Arizona State University's *Research* magazine. He now works as a freelance illustrator/designer and fine artist.

Jean Kilker is a teacher-librarian and former Follett Librarian of the Year. She applied her experience in teaching language arts, reading and science to develop the curriculum guide for *AZWOWW*.

Linda F. Radke, president of Five Star Publications, Inc., applies over 26 years of publishing, marketing, writing experience and ingenuity to ensure value and quality for *AZWOWW*.

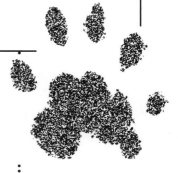

85 Farm Seek (Hidden Objects)

27 Plants and Animals

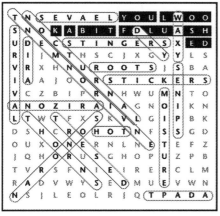

71 Jail Tree

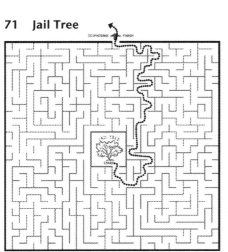

93 Counting On Arizona

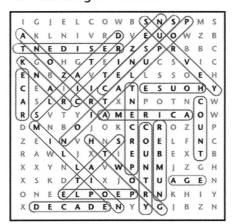

A Resource for Every Author & Publisher Since 1985

Sensational Centennial Reads

Five Star Publications' *Arizona Way Out West & Wacky*, *Arizona Way Out West & Witty: Library Edition*, *Arizona Color Me Wacky!*, *Addie Slaughter: The Girl Who Met Geronimo* and *Cheery: The True Adventures of a Chiricahua Leopard Frog* are all designated Arizona Centennial Legacy Project books. Purchase them online at www.FiveStarPublications.com; click on "Bookstore."

To book the authors for a school visit, call 480-940-8182 or email info@FiveStarPublications.com.

Arizona Way Out West & Wacky! This 112-page book is ideal for grades K-6, offering hours of fun through true, but humorous, gross, interesting and wacky stories and facts about Arizona. PLUS: crossword puzzles, coloring pages, games, recipes, crafts, word searches and brain busters!

Arizona: Color Me Wacky! Born out of the wildly successful *Arizona Way Out West & Wacky*, *Arizona Color Me Wacky!* features 32 pages of coloring fun. The text teaches children about the Grand Canyon State's unique animals, plants and insects. The delightful, yet scientifically correct illustrations were created by award-winning illustrator Michael Hagelberg.

Arizona Way Out West & Witty: Library Edition (Chapter Book) This 116-page *ONEBOOK for Kids 2012* winner is ideal for grades 4 to adult, offering all the same entertaining and educational tales as *Arizona Way Out West & Wacky*, as well as puzzles, games, recipes, crafts and brain busters! EXCEPT *AZ-Witty* is not designed to be written in. PLUS, it includes a curriculum guide!

ONEBOOKAZ *For Kids* 2012 WINNER

Addie Slaughter: The Girl Who Met Geronimo, tells the true story of Sheriff John Slaughter's young daughter. In the late-1800s, she bravely travels from Texas to the Slaughter Ranch on the Arizona-Mexico border. On her journey her mother dies; she narrowly escapes from a stagecoach robbery and murder; the ranch is destroyed by earthquake; her father's earlobe is shot off; and she meets with Geronimo. Visit www.AddieSlaughterBook.com.

Cheery: The true adventures of a Chiricahua Leopard Frog lets children read the story of this little creature growing from tadpole to frog. They learn why many kinds of frogs around the world, including those like Cheery, are dramatically declining in numbers. Visit www.CheeryAFrogsTale.com.

www.AZWOWW.com | www.AddieSlaughterBook.com | www.CheeryAFrogsTale.com